Judith
Enjoy ...
thanks for ...
Veterans

MW00761204

Facing The Wall:
An Infantryman's
Post-Vietnam Memoir

Phil Ferrazano

Phil Ferrazano

11-9-18

Booklocker.com, Inc.
2003

Cover art by Darrell King, www.pixelmonkey.net.
Edited by Janice Strand, www.JaniceStrand.com.

For questions about the book or reprint requests, contact:

Phil Ferrazano
1472 Canterbury Drive
Clearwater, FL 33756
Email: Phil@FacingTheWall.com

Dedication

I HAVE SO MANY people to thank, and my gratitude extends far beyond the pages of this book. First, thanks to my ex-wife Kathleen for her devotion and love for thirty years, not only for me, but my comrades. She blessed me with a daughter and gave me the courage to tell our story. She too, is a hero of the battle. I'll always be grateful for what she gave me in life.

My daughter Michelle has been an inspiration to me. Her love for her dad has lifted my spirits over and over. She's been my purpose in life. She has been a pleasure and a blessing, and she's made me very proud. I'll love her always.

Evelyn found me when I was lost. She has made me appreciative of what I have in life, and she made me love again. I thank her for sharing her love, zest for life, and the dance. Her love for me has made me sing again.

Thanks go to my mom and dad, sisters and brother, for always being there for me, and for loving me as their son and brother.

Special thanks go to Bob and Linda Wilson for their friendship through some hard times. Linda's computer skills and long hours of typing that first draft from my handwritten script helped bring my story to life.

Award-winning artist Darrell King volunteered his time and immeasurable talents to create my book cover. Thank you, guy, for using your art to help a veteran.

I also want to give thanks to Janice Strand. You're a very gifted and talented editor, writer, and author. You shared your knowledge of your craft with me. Even more importantly, you embraced my story with passion and a deep understanding. Let's not forget how many chocolate chip cookies you baked, either. Thanks, Janice.

Of course none of this would have started without Joe Adcock, who first encouraged me to put my story down on paper, to help myself and others who would follow after me. Thanks, Joe.

I also want to thank the VA doctors and nurses who have helped me. There are many who dedicate themselves to provide the best care they can. Even though government policies seem to stand in their way, they always seem to give that little extra to help the veterans.

Finally, thanks to my comrades who fought with me in Vietnam. Their love for me as a brother in battle will always be remembered, just as I'll remember my lost brothers whose names grace The Wall.

Foreword

Joseph B. Adcock, MA
Former Captain, USMC,
Vietnam Readjustment Counseling Therapist,
VA Vet Center Program (Retired)

PHIL FERRAZANO'S GROUNDBREAKING book *Facing The Wall* is not your typical Vietnam veteran's memoir. Although he does take you back to one of the most tumultuous times in American history, the core struggle in the book is one of post-war survival. Phil's story resonates not only with Vietnam veterans, but with all of us who have endured war.

With great insight, honesty and openness, he provides a path to recovery from one of the worst tragedies humankind has ever faced. He does so with grace and dignity. The miracle of this book is that there is no miraculous ending. The miracle of this book is that by sharing his pain and suffering—his struggle to accept the hand he'd been dealt, fighting for the health care and compensation he rightfully earned and deserved—Phil found a measure of peace with himself, his family, and his god.

During Phil's pilgrimage to find self-worth, self-respect, and a reason to live despite continuing losses in his life, he discovered he needed to focus on his first loves—his family, his talents, and his relationship with his god. He learned that his talents of storytelling, speaking, songwriting, and singing touch others' lives in ways he never imagined. The result was an overwhelming drive to share his story with countless combat veterans who have endured similar post-war injustices.

The best way to honor those lost in battle is to minister to others about the true horrors of the aftermath of armed conflict, both during times of peace and times of conflict.

Phil's pilgrimage forced him to face the mental and emotional anguish he experienced in war while enduring tremendous physical pain. Through this process he achieved peace. Those who follow Phil's path, enduring the challenges of the pilgrimage with an open and persistent spirit, may find their own rewards—a calm mind, a mended heart, and a renewed soul.

Phil came to terms with the tragedies of war, facing the difficult questions that haunt so many other veterans. Why did I survive when others didn't? In the aftermath of such enormous manmade death and destruction, what is the meaning of life? Where do I go from here? Can I endure the system long enough to receive what is due me? What then is my purpose and direction in life? Riddled with scars of body and spirit, am I still of value? Can I once again be of worth to humankind?

I lived this process with Phil. What began as an exercise in therapeutic journaling became his life's journey—a compelling tale of battles won and lost. Most importantly, Phil's story is one of self-redemption through determined perseverance.

Persistence was key to Phil's struggle. Sadly, America's provisions for caring for those who have borne the burdens of battle do not always include treating our warriors with the dignity, respect, and benefits they have earned.

As a readjustment counseling therapist who worked with vets for over twenty-five years, I have always been amazed at how some veterans are treated with such care and compassion and others are not. Although there are some very dedicated and compassionate people who really care about the veterans they serve, indifference, lack of compassion and unfairness often plague veterans. Too often health care providers turn on their patients, blaming them for the VA health care's failures. As in

Phil's case, the VA compensation system seems eager to discredit injuries and illnesses that did in fact occur as a result of military service. This disturbing burden unnecessarily adds to the pain and suffering our veterans have already endured for their country. Phil's experiences are not isolated. There are many more—more than I wish to acknowledge.

Facing the Wall is a story whose time has come. It is very timely in view of this generation of combat veterans coming home from Iraq. Let us hope the U.S. government does not repeat failures of past wars. Let us insist that this generation of combatants is treated better than those who have gone before them.

This book should be required reading for every American—every congressman who has ever voted on legislation affecting veterans, every VA employee who has ever been frustrated by their inability to help a veteran, every citizen who lived through this horrific period in America's past, and most importantly, every American who hadn't yet been born when the warriors of Vietnam were slogging through the jungle for their country. We must never repeat the failures of the past.

Joseph B. Adcock, MA
Former Captain, USMC, Vietnam
Readjustment Counseling Therapist
VA Vet Center Program (Retired)

The Moving Wall

I never thought you'd come to see me, in my hometown.
What the hell, I should have known you'd never let me down.
You were young, free, and full of life, you all.
Oh let those tears fall at The Wall.
When the sun beats up against you, I can see those smiles
Even though I left you back so many miles.
You're the real heroes now; you let us stand tall.
After all, it's written, and they put you on a wall. So move on
now;
You know your job will never be done.
You're a husband, brother, buddy, and son.
You have to be shared by everyone.

—Phil Ferrazano

Chapter One

TWENTY YEARS AFTER I left Vietnam, I realized the war still hadn't ended for me. It took an unending mirror of black granite to help me understand.

I had always intended on seeing The Moving Wall, the half-size Vietnam Veterans Memorial that traveled the country carrying the names of over 58,000 dead soldiers, including ten of my friends. The memorial had been in St. Petersburg, Florida for a week, but I waited until the last day to face those names.

The afternoon sun hung low in the sky when I arrived at the site of the memorial. I was here to pay homage to the men who died in this illegitimate war, and yet I couldn't make myself approach. I detoured to a tent where patient workers helped me locate the names of my comrades.

I looked at the list and half-wondered why my name wasn't on it as well. Part of me died in that war. Shouldn't my name be between Bunny's and Washington's?

The wall seemed to both draw me in and repel me. Its somber depths pulled me close, but my memories couldn't bring me near enough to read the names I sought.

On the ground a man sat in his old Army fatigues. They were worn and weathered, like the man. He stared at The Wall, transfixed. I wanted to say something to him. What, I wasn't sure.

"It's a bitch man," he said, more to himself than to me.

"I was with the 9th," I said in a low voice.

His eyes sparked with recognition, or perhaps with the

relief of having someone to distract him from The Wall. "Yeah, down in the delta, right?" he asked. "I was with the First Cavalry."

I nodded and my gaze drifted back to The Wall. Silence engulfed us.

"Can't walk up, man," he said finally. He looked up at me, searching. His pain was one I shared.

"You don't have to," I said. "They know you're here, and they know you care." I rested my hand on his shoulder and he nodded with downcast eyes.

The words meant to absolve a stranger had released me as well. I knew I didn't have to read the names to honor my friends. But I knew now that I could.

I took a deep breath and searched for the first name on the list.

Staff Sergeant Robert Washington had been in his second tour when he was killed. He died the night I had received the shrapnel I still carried in my head and shoulders. The constant pain from those wounds was nothing compared to the pain Washington's wife and four kids must have gone through.

A middle-aged woman stood next to her teenage son. "There's your daddy's name," she said.

The teenage boy gently rubbed his fingers across the name of the father he never knew. His mother's lips trembled as she fought back the tears, and then she resigned herself. She wrapped her arms around her son and tears tumbled down both their faces.

Phil Orgeron was the next name. Our lives had been similar. We got the most care packages from home with plenty of chocolate chip cookies, Velveeta cheese and peanut butter to share with all the guys. I swallowed hard as I visualized the young, good-looking guy from Louisiana, smiling and joking around. He was so proud of his girlfriend. They were to be married as soon as he got back home.

It hurt when I tried to remember the picture of her he always carried with him. A bright smile and curls down the middle of her back. How had losing Phil affected her? Dark, tearful eyes and a heart filled with pain? Was that how my wife had felt when she heard of my injury?

I wanted to leave. Each moment became harder and harder to bear. Yet I wanted to go on. I owed this to them, and to myself.

I searched for another name, Private First Class William Bunting. We called him Bunny. It fit; he was gentle and sensitive, and wouldn't hurt a soul. Not good personality traits for a soldier. When he had arrived in country he needed a protector. I helped him along the best I could.

Staff Sergeant Dale Williams had been *my* protector. He was the best soldier I'd ever met and took me under his wing. I wanted to mourn for him, but part of me was angry—with *him*, because he had let himself get killed.

"Why man, why am I looking at your name on this wall?" I whispered. I touched his name and bowed my head. "This shouldn't have happened."

When he died I still had seven months left in Vietnam. I tried to erase his memory. If a seasoned soldier could be killed, what kind of odds had I had?

Even now, so many years later, when I finally had the chance to mourn for my old friend, it was still hard. How could someone so young and full of life die?

I read his name over and over again on The Wall. It must be true; this somber, black monument confirmed it.

Then something different pried its way through my tears of confusion.

Anger. No, rage.

Something was going on inside of me, twenty years after I last set foot in that hell hole.

Why now?

Myriad emotions screamed for my attention. Guilt—why was I here, and not them? Shame—had I done something, lived a life less honorable that allowed me to escape? Anger—oh, this was the big one. I was angry at myself for living, them for dying, and the government for sending us there. Disgust—would the government ever acknowledge, or even realize, the horrors they had thrust upon so many young men?

I had my own share of horrors. I suffered from blinding headaches, as well as shrapnel wounds to the back, shoulder, and head. Yet I couldn't complain about this as I stood before The Wall. These men had paid the ultimate price in service to their country. Who was I to whine about a few injuries? I was still alive. I would be around to see my daughter graduate from high school, get married, and maybe even have kids of her own. It was an acceptable trade-off—a few wounds for a life. The men on that wall had been given no such option.

The next name was Carl Crowe, a sergeant in my company. He was like that favorite uncle who always knew how to make you laugh. He bitched about the Army, but he stayed in. He was killed on a day when he shouldn't even have been in the field. He was "short," with only a little time left in country. He was hit with shrapnel and went into shock and died. The old man of the company had died at thirty-eight. He served his country, did the twenty years, and died just weeks short of retirement. Where was the justice in that? What god would have let this—all of this—happen?

Memories flashed through my mind like a newsreel. Too much, too fast. Still, The Wall drew me to it.

The next name was RTO Jon Sapp, a radio telephone operator, like myself, and the first GI that I saw killed. Hell, we had both been walking targets. No matter where the division went we had to be there, but instead of the comforting cold metal of a rifle, we got that damnable handset buzzing in our ears.

"No wonder I never could sleep," I mumbled. My heart thudded in my chest and sweat poured down my face, the hot Florida sun obscuring the tears. Even the relentless July heat reminded me of that hellhole.

Next were two childhood friends, Jimmy Lewis and Mike Murphy. Jimmy was my age, the class of 1968. A short, muscular guy, I remember cutting up with him in music class only a short time before he went over. He was a tough kid with a lot of friends—the kind of guy you thought could never get hurt.

Mike Murphy had been my Boy Scout senior patrol leader. When I was fourteen he was the guy we all looked up to and wanted to be like. He went off to Vietnam before I even started growing pubic hair. Died before I got there myself.

"How long did this piece of shit war last anyway?" I mumbled.

My stomach rolled when I realized Vietnam had dogged me through my entire teen years, and then beyond.

In high school we feared being sent into battle if we didn't go to college, but we also feared the guilt we knew we'd feel if we tried to avoid our duty to God and our country.

I remembered when John Kennedy was shot and killed. Graphic pictures flashed across a black and white television stuck in my young mind. *He* was a World War II hero. *He* did the right thing. It's what so many of us felt we should do.

But before I graduated high school, John Kennedy's little brother was assassinated.

Kids grew up watching John Wayne in *The Sands Of Iwo Jima* and *The Green Berets*. Going to war was honorable, and right, we were taught.

But was it?

So many years later, I was reliving those doubts of my 1968 senior year. Looking back, should I have tried for college, or the border?

The Wall reaffirmed the decision I had made long ago.

"Hell no!" I said, not caring who heard. "Hell no."

It had been my fate, my duty to be with these guys. I had the privilege to serve with the best and the bravest men. They were right, and they died doing a job for their country. They never knew the outcome, but it didn't matter. The war ended for them on a tangled jungle floor somewhere, covered in mud and blood. For the rest of us, it lived on. Every day the pain in my shoulder and the vise-like migraines reminded me of how the war continued to flourish.

My temper flared and I paced angrily away. I needed a break—from the heat, from The Wall, and from my own memories. I had to stop thinking about my own personal situation—my mistreatment from Army doctors and the Veteran's Administration. I wasn't at The Wall for that. I was only here to see my lost buddies' names and pay my respects. It was way overdue.

I stood beneath a live oak tree dripping with Spanish moss. A newsman gestured his cameraman towards me. "Over here," he said.

The camera rolled and the newsman Scott Rapport—who later went on to work for *Inside Edition*—held a microphone to my face.

"What are you feeling?" Scott asked.

I had to pause for a moment before I could say anything.

"I hope they didn't die in vain. I want to believe they had a purpose," I replied.

The camera stopped.

"You're going to be on the news, guy. What's your name?" he asked as he bummed a cigarette off his cameraman.

"Phil Ferrazano."

He jotted it down on a notepad. "Well, Phil, I've been trying for the last hour to capture the true sentiment of a Vietnam veteran. Thanks."

I nodded and gave my approval with a grin.

He smiled and we shook hands. The firmness of his grip convinced me that The Wall was affecting him too. I was glad.

I turned back to The Wall feeling a bit more comfortable.

"I knew you'd be here," a voice said from behind me. I felt a solid hand on my back.

"Hey John!" I yelled, turning and clasping the hand of a stout, blond-haired man with an eager grin.

John and I had hung around throughout high school and then again when I first came home. When he got divorced, we lost contact.

"I'm living right around the corner now," he said. "I had the feeling you'd be here today."

I smiled. "It's good to see you."

"A lot of guys we know up there," John said, gesturing towards The Wall.

"Yeah," I said. "Kids. We were all just kids."

"I wish I had gone with you," John said, his body stiffening. He had chosen college over 'Nam.

"Don't. You did what was right for you," I said. "It just wasn't right for me. I guess I watched one too many episodes of *Combat* to stay home." I grinned.

"Vic Morrow to the end, huh?" John's shoulders slumped and he relaxed as he grinned back at me. Even those who didn't go to Vietnam had scars that needed healing. We parted, but promised to stay in touch. I headed home to my wife and daughter.

The day had drained me. When I stepped into my pickup truck and drove away, I felt as if I had been on a mission back in 'Nam.

I glanced back at The Wall one last time. It had been hard to greet that unwelcome traveler. Little did I know that the worst was yet to come.

Today was to be a turning point in my life. Feelings I had

buried so deeply had begun to surface. I had to deal with them, even though after twenty years I hadn't a clue about how to start.

I knew I was searching for something. Peace? Respect? I wasn't sure, but I felt something change inside of me that day. I had taken my first steps on a journey that would transport me from my comfortable home in Clearwater, Florida back to the jungles Vietnam, and forward into an uncertain future of pain and betrayal.

The journey had begun.

Chapter Two

ONE SUFFOCATING AFTERNOON on patrol in the Vietnam jungle we passed monks in a village. Their reverent chanting chilled me. Their high, rolling tones were punctuated by the ringing of a deep, echoing bell—and our contribution, the clatter of slung rifles.

"What do you think they're praying for?" I asked my buddy Bill.

"For us," he answered.

"You really think so?"

"Yeah," Bill said, a rueful smile crossing his smudged face. "They're praying we'll suffer forever for fighting in Vietnam."

So many years later, it felt as if it were true. Those of us who entered their country had suffered for it. There was no doubt about that.

When I came back from Vietnam in 1971 I brought with me a head and chest full of shrapnel and migraines that shadowed my every attempt at a normal life.

As time went on, my pain became worse and I started going to the VA hospital for medical attention. I got lots of pills, but not much in the way of answers. What was causing the pain I woke up to every morning, and went to bed with every night?

Requests for diagnostic tests were met with excuses and bureaucracy. Most doctors didn't seem concerned with what I'd explain to them and I quickly became very tired of repeating my story. If they asked about my experiences in combat, I'd resent it. I felt I didn't need to explain anything to anybody. My wounds were my proof.

Those without wounds couldn't possibly understand what I was going through. I knew this first-hand. Before I had gone to Vietnam, I had been just like they were. We all had been. We took our lives for granted. If it didn't concern us we just didn't care that much.

"Oh, just make believe you were never wounded, or that you even went to Vietnam. You'll be all right," one doctor told me.

His comment, and others like it, ate at me. I'd toss and turn at night in anger. The uncaring words of doctors cut through me worse than the wounds themselves. I had a new enemy. I was at war again, but this time I vowed to be the winner.

I wanted payback.

✪ ✪ ✪

SEEKING MEDICAL ATTENTION as a wounded veteran was difficult. You were assigned a disability rating based on the perceived degree of your injury. Thirty percent for a missing foot, maybe forty percent if the whole leg was gone. Benefits and access to medical treatment increased with your percentage. Seeking help was often believed to be an attempt to simply boost your rating.

Reaching 100 percent disability put you in a totally different category, but to get there, the system put you through the ringer. Many deserving veterans never reached that high before they gave up or died, from their wounds—or from their own hands.

I popped pills constantly. Many of them upset my stomach and made me groggy. The doctors eventually performed a temporary nerve block that left my left rib area with a pins and needles sensation. They wanted to do a permanent one but I refused. I figured pain was a signal that something was wrong, and masking it might camouflage the source.

And the pain continued to grow. The poor treatment I received at the hands of my doctors triggered haunting thoughts of Vietnam. I was battling anew, but I felt just as powerless as I had in 'Nam.

One doctor did state that I had nerve damage from shrapnel and advised me to put in for more disability. My wounds had formed scar tissue in my chest wall. The scar tissue was probably pushing on nerves and causing the pain. It made sense.

Two years later I had an exam for an increase. It took five minutes and consisted mainly of moving up and down and bending. The pain was excruciating, but the VA doesn't pay for pain, so again I was denied.

I continued on with the construction business I owned, but found myself becoming more and more obsessed with the past. It started with the helicopters. Each time one would fly overhead, I found myself back into the Mekong.

I'd talk for hours on the phone with my friend Dan. We had been drafted together and flew to 'Nam on the same plane. We both served in the 9th Division. We talked about our problems, about the anger that welled up inside of us each time we thought about our mistreatment. After a while we decided we both needed help and sought out the local Vet Center. Two visits and we were convinced it wasn't for us. Listening to other veterans' war stories just pissed us off.

✪ ✪ ✪

I CONTINUED TO SEEK help for my wounds. I made an appointment at the VA hospital over in Tampa.

The doctor I saw didn't greet me, shake my hand— nothing. "What's wrong with you?" she asked brusquely, her nose buried in a folder. She never even looked me in the eyes.

I hated the way she added "with you" at the end of her question. VA doctors often did that. It meant they thought you were just another complainer, someone looking to boost their disability rating. I was sure their job was to keep veterans from having grounds for a claim.

The doctor had a thick Middle Eastern accent and it made me feel I was telling my story to a stranger, a foreigner, who couldn't possibly understand my situation. It made me uncomfortable and defensive.

"There's a burning feeling underneath my wound, under my left shoulder blade, almost in the center of my back. It bores through my chest," I said.

She didn't comment.

"It also hurts in my ribs. It makes it tough to lift or pull, and that's what I do at my job. I own a construction company." I loved my work, but more importantly, I had a family and I needed to support them. I did right by my country when I served. Now they needed to do right by me.

"No way!" she snapped.

"I know what the pain is that I'm feeling!" I shouted back.

She grabbed my arm and pulled down on it. "Now lift!" she said.

I did. "So what the hell does that prove?" I asked.

She wrote out a script for extra strength Tylenol and left without a word.

The blood rushed to my head as if the top of my head would explode—instant migraine. I carried my records down to a desk. No one wanted to take them. I threw them at the clerk.

"I'll never come back to this place," I yelled, storming out.

✪ ✪ ✪

LEAVING THE HOSPITAL didn't mean that the pain had left

my body. After a few months I decided to try the pain management class offered at the VA hospital closer to my house.

I attended three sessions and skipped the fourth. I had the feeling that they wanted me to believe that all the pain was in my head. I still had shrapnel in my body, and the scars to prove it. It didn't seem to matter.

After my missed session I received a call from a young intern who had been involved with the class.

"You missed the class," she said. "I'd like to have you come in to talk, one on one."

I agreed and we made an appointment for the following week. When we met again, asked questions about Vietnam, my childhood, family, and work—everything they always asked me. But she had showed she cared about me, more than anyone else so far, and I opened up to her. The emotions I felt at The Wall came pouring out.

"Phil, I think you have post-traumatic stress disorder," she said.

"What?" Post-traumatic stress disorder conjured images of disheveled street people mumbling about the jungle from within their cardboard boxes.

"You've hidden it well."

"But I've got my business, and a family that loves me. I'm—"

"Functioning," she finished. "That's all you're doing, Phil. You're getting by—and much better than so many of the vets I see through here—but you've never taken time to confront your feelings about that time.

"You also have physical problems that are a result of your wounds and that only complicates things."

I looked down and shook my head. Did my thoughts about Vietnam have that much power over me? Was this why for years I couldn't get a good night's sleep? About my anger—

was it possible this was causing my pain?

This couldn't be happening to me. I wasn't weak. I had made it out of the 'Nam.

Or had I?

"Please try the Vet Center again," the intern said. "It's changed since the last time you were there. I'll even call for you. You'll meet with Joe Adcock, a 'Nam vet, just like you. And you should consider going to the stress recovery unit here at the hospital."

How could a young woman in her twenties show more compassion for what I faced in Vietnam than all the doctors I had faced in the past? It hurt me to think that perhaps the country had been so divided over the war that those of my generation simply didn't care.

"You should be service connected for PTSD, along with your other problems," she continued.

I was at a loss for words. I didn't even know there was a rating for post-traumatic stress disorder and I hadn't ever heard of the stress unit.

Later that day I called the Vet Center. They had already received a call from the intern and said they were looking forward to me coming down.

They cared, and I wasn't used to it.

Cautious but hopeful, a few days later I walked up a wooden ramp that lead into an old house that served as the Vet Center.

"Hi, can I help you?" asked a very polite black lady as I entered uncharted waters.

"Yes. I'm here to see Mr. Adcock. My name is Phil Ferrazano."

"Oh yes, he'll see you in a minute. Please take a seat over there," she said, pointing to what must have been the parlor or living room of the place when it had been a home. The room had comfortable couches and chairs set in little clusters around a fireplace. Mementos of Vietnam were scattered about—pictures, unit patches, and even a glass display case of medals.

"Thanks," I replied back with a smile. *Not bad so far*, I thought.

After a few minutes, the door next to the front desk opened and a tall, slender man, well groomed with glasses, strode over to greet me.

"Hi, Phil. I'm Joe. Please come in."

I followed him into his office and took a seat in an oversized blue armchair—the hot seat.

Joe gently closed the door behind us. His office was obviously that of a busy man, but I sensed no urgency in Joe's tone or demeanor. Three Vietnam hats covered with unit patches filled a shelf next to my chair—proof that he was a fellow vet.

"So how can I help?" said Joe.

"Well, I was told I might be suffering with PTSD and that I should see you," I said reluctantly. So many years had past and now I was crying the blues about Vietnam? What would this stern-looking ex-marine captain think of me?

He focused on me and leaned forward. "Yeah, I got a call." He put his hands to his chin. "We'll have to meet a few times. We'll talk about your background. For today, though, just a couple of basic questions. When were you in 'Nam?"

"From February 1970 until the end of January 1971."

He nodded his head as he looked around for a blank piece of paper. He took notes as he spoke.

"You were infantry, right?"

"Yes sir, the 9th Division. I was a RTO, a radio telephone operator." I gulped and continued quickly. "I was wounded in Cambodia." I wanted him to know I had every right to be sitting in that seat.

"Okay Phil, I'd like to set up a few appointments so I can really get the feel of what's going on with you. Next week I'd like to meet with you for about an hour, okay?"

"Sure, what day?"

"Let me look," he said as he thumbed through a calendar that looked like a crossword puzzle.

To me it seemed appropriate. It was all starting to feel like a puzzle, but with pieces missing. Would Joe be the one to help me find them?

✪ ✪ ✪

MY HANDS SWELLED and ached. My work suffered. I needed hospital care. Even more, I needed answers. The Vet Center was a start, but maybe I did need a visit to that stress unit. It would be hard to be away from my family and business for the two months they required, but maybe taking time out for me was what I needed.

If I was staying in the hospital, they would have to run tests, wouldn't they? I had to find out why I hurt so badly.

I began to wind down my business. I couldn't work now with my hands swelling anyway. It was about time I got some results and the VA should help me. I wasn't a shiftless slacker; I'd been working over twenty years with the pain from shrapnel wounds my constant companion. It didn't seem fair.

✪ ✪ ✪

AT MY NEXT appointment with Joe, he asked me to tell him about my days in Cambodia. My mind slipped back in time.

We were on a patrol through some pretty dense jungle, walking single file. I was around the middle in back of Three-Six, my lieutenant.

My ear was to the horn as usual. I had just made battalion RTO, so I was nervous. It was a lot of responsibility. This mission made everyone scared.

Cambodia was so green and lush. From the helicopter it seemed like a paradise. Once on the ground, the illusion was shattered. It was nothing but mud and blood and guts and gooks in the underbrush.

Around our sixth day in Cambodia, we went off on patrol. Each platoon set out in a different direction. It was just after midday as we began our patrol. Suddenly the German shepherd scout dog smelled something. He started to run, but his trainer held him back.

"Come on!" yelled Three-Six.

Without thinking, I followed him into a large clearing, shooting as I ran—thirty, maybe forty feet.

Directly into an enemy camp.

In the clearing, NVA soldiers lounged around a smoldering cooking fire. Others slept in hammocks, totally unaware.

But we were as surprised to see them as they were to see us. Three-Six and I braced ourselves against a bamboo fence. We had our own personal shooting gallery of enemy soldiers.

I felt sick with every squeeze of the trigger.

"Shoot! Shoot!" ordered Three-Six as he frantically sprayed his M-16 on full automatic.

I chose semi-automatic; that's what the guys who had been in country the longest had told me. More control, less ammo wasted. The rest of the squad hadn't made it into the clearing before the NVA began returning fire. We were cut off.

I was doing what was right, but each time one of my rounds made those hammocks spin and splatter blood, I didn't feel like it.

We were shooting, shoulder to shoulder, only two feet apart.

Then Three-Six wasn't shooting.

As I changed magazines, I glanced over at Three-Six. He dropped slowly to the ground.

His M-16 barrel pointed toward his face. His head slouched to the right and I saw the bullet hole on the right side of his nose.

Sniper.

My world stopped—no breeze, still, quiet, no feelings. No words could explain what I felt at that very moment.

A bullet burned my arm and I dropped to the ground to help my wounded lieutenant. I pulled him closer to the fence. I needed to get us both out of the view of the asshole sniper crouching somewhere in the trees.

What the hell was I going to do now? What the hell kind of bullshit training was going to get me out of this one?

"Medic!" I screamed at the top of my lungs.

No one could get to us. In a heartbeat we had gone from us holding the upper hand to them. Bullets flew all around us.

I screamed into the handset of my radio. "Need a dust off, Three-Six is hit! I'm pinned down!"

"Give me your coordinates," Jackson, the guy on the other end, said.

I did.

"Can't be there," he said.

"What?" I screamed.

We were lost. Three-Six's map didn't have our current position. We had drifted off course, or maybe we were just plain lost.

Later I found out that Three-Six had led us off course in search of a watering hole. We were all hot and tired, and plunging into some cool water would have been wonderful for his men. He only thought of them. He had no way of knowing what he was leading us into, or that drifting off course might have cost him his life.

I called the captain. They were in a firefight. All platoons were in contact. We were in the middle of a damn regiment of North Vietnamese Army.

"Oh man!" I yelled over the radio, screaming for a medic.

Minutes later, our medic dashed toward us. Doc Izard was the bravest little son of bitch I've ever seen. Bullets danced all around him. I could see the dirt fly at his feet. He zigzagged till he hit the ground next to me.

Bill and Bunny, my buddies, crawled out of the wood line and shot into the trees, laying down fire for the doc.

The rest of the guys made it around to the soldier in the tree and blew the hell out of him and the tree.

I spotted a loach, an observation chopper, flying high off into the distance.

"Find out who it is and get me a frequency!" I screamed to Jackson.

He did. It was a colonel flying around.

"I need a dust off. Three-Six is hit!" I demanded.

"Calm down son," he replied.

Bullets struck all around me. "Goddamn it, my lieutenant is hit in the fucking head! Get me a chopper. I can't calm down!" I yelled back.

Sergeant Ski made it to us and relieved me from the horn. Exhausted, I talked to Three-Six. He didn't look like he would make it. A bullet in the head—it was serious.

We popped a smoke grenade and they spotted us, but each time the medivac chopper came towards us, it took fire and had to fly away. We were too deep into their territory. Too many snipers. We never saw the men who shot at us.

The chopper finally made it to the ground on its third attempt. We dragged Three-Six to it and loaded him in. I wasn't sure if I'd ever see him again.

Chapter Three

JOE WAS THE first person I had told Three-Six's story to in such detail. That night I couldn't sleep. I didn't want to think about it again. I had tried to force the events from my mind. After more than twenty years, I realized I'd done nothing but the opposite. I thought about Vietnam every day, the good days and the bad, from morning until night, at every meal, taking a shower or driving the car. My memories haunted me.

It was after midnight and I was still wide awake. I clicked the TV on and fiddled with the remote. I kept the volume low, not wanting to wake my wife and daughter.

I stopped when I saw a Vietnam War scene. Late at night there was always something on about 'Nam. Within ten minutes it had me in tears. And like always, I wasn't sad. I was angry.

"This stuff is taking me over," I said aloud. "I'm stronger than this, right?" I felt the war had changed me. But shouldn't I have changed back, after I came home?

But I didn't. None of my friends did either. Getting your ass shot at did that to you. I had to watch a buddy blown apart. I spent nights in a miserable swamp with mosquitoes so big they could almost carry you away.

"But the Plain of Reeds was such a *nice* goddamned place!" I laughed.

"I'm crazy," I said to the quiet house.

I walked over to the kitchen, pulled open a drawer and fumbled around, praying for a bottle of Tylenol with codeine to end the pain. I popped two even though I knew I should only take one.

"The hell with it," I said. I was hoping it would knock me out.

My mind couldn't help but drift back to July 1970. Tan An, 9th Division headquarters. I had a job on the bunker line a couple of months after I was wounded.

✪ ✪ ✪

I WAS SITTING ON guard duty in the middle of the night with two close friends, Chris and Dave. We all called Dave "Redman" because of his dark red hair. How many companies must have had guys named Red? They all did. Hell, we all had nicknames.

The three of us were wounded and assigned to this unit. It wasn't bad and it sure beat the hell out of the field. But I still couldn't escape the pounding migraine headaches. Tonight's was particularly bad.

My friends would often witness my pain and they'd help me as much as they could. Some would even pull my guard duties when I couldn't.

"You got screwed man! Your ass should have been sent home," Chris said.

Chris and I became close friends after I was wounded. One of my squad buddies Bill had gone to high school with him back in the States. I missed Bill and worried about him all the time. At times I felt lucky I got hit. Guys were shooting each other in the feet just to get out. Some even talked of suicide.

"I'm taking you to the aid station," Chris said. The aid station was a barracks set up for medical needs.

"Yeah," piped Redman.

Redman had a buzz on from a few too many beers before he came up to the watchtower.

Suddenly I felt what little gruel I had put in my stomach

that night fight its way up my throat and onto the floor.

"That's it," Chris said. He got on the horn to advise the bunker guard next door he had to get me over to the aid station. "Bunker three, this is bunker four. Over."

"Roger that, four. We'll cover for you. Let me know when you're back."

"Let's go man. You're sick. Maybe you can get out of this place."

Chris looked out for me. He didn't like seeing guys getting screwed over, especially wounded grunts. He hated the Army.

I leaned on Redman and Chris as we stumbled into the aid station where a major was sitting at a desk eating an apple.

"My buddy is sick as hell," Chris said. "He was wounded in the head and has had severe headaches ever since," said Chris.

For a moment the major on duty didn't say a word, just ate his apple and flipped through his damn magazine. He looked up and spoke in broken English. "What do you want me to do about it?"

"Are you kidding me man?" Chris replied back with his mouth open.

Redman chuckled in disbelief. I stood there ready to turn the major's spit-shined boots into puke-shined ones.

"I can only give him some aspirin, that is it."

"Up yours!" I cried through the pain. "Aspirins don't help!" I was ready to kill this rear echelon mother fucker.

I knew I was out of line, but I couldn't help it. My vision blurred and my eyes were ready to explode from my head.

"Who do you think you're talking to?" he crowed, spitting apple as he talked. "I'll have your ass!"

"I don't care. You call yourself a doctor? You'd better stay in this man's Army because you'll never get a job on the outside!"

I wanted to choke the guy. I really didn't care what he was

going to do with me.

"Put me in jail," I said.

His eyes bulged out in astonishment. Lowly E-4s never talked to majors like I was. Never.

Fuck him. I had a Combat Infantryman Badge and a Purple Heart. What did this guy contribute to the damn place? Infantry officers had more respect for me than they did for this major; I was sure of that.

I was sick and he wasn't doing his job. He didn't care about me or any other poor bastard that spent time in the bush.

"Let's get the hell out of here!" I said.

The major sat there dumbfounded with a blank look on his face, the half-eaten apple still half-raised to his mouth.

Chris and Redman took me by the arms and carried me out.

"I can't believe you talked to an officer like that," said Redman laughing.

"Whoa! I hope he doesn't report you," said Chris.

"No way," I said. "It's our word against his. He'd be afraid we'd frag him. Then he'd be out his government pension." I stumbled and the guys caught me. "I can't get over that guy. He could care less."

"Yeah, you're right buddy," Chris said. "He won't say a word. He's too worried about his own hide."

They took me back to the bunker and stayed up all night with me. We only had each other. If you were sick no one cared. At least I had guys with me who had also been wounded. They had an idea what I was going through. Some only figured you were avoiding the field.

No kidding! If you got your ass shot up why the hell would you be expected to go back out? Unless of course you were crazy enough to want to. And there were enough who did. They didn't need my hurting, jumpy body on line. I did my time on line and did it damn well. I hated the thought of getting another chance at death.

✪ ✪ ✪

STARTING TO FEEL the effects of the codeine, I shut the
television off. I headed for the bed trying to keep my eyes
closed so I could fall asleep. Kathy was out like a light. I
crawled into my side of the bed not wanting to wake her.

Too many nights when I was suffering with a bad
migraine, she'd had to sit up with me, or even drive me to an
emergency room because the pain was so bad.

Always the same. Shrapnel in his head and chest? Get him
the hell out of here. Tell him to go to the VA.

I closed my eyes and begged for sleep to come and
vanquish my thoughts.

✪ ✪ ✪

EVEN DURING THE day my memories haunted me. But it
was different now. I was searching them out just as they sought
me. I knew I had to dig deeper to get to the root of my
emotions.

I knew some of it had to do with getting wounded and not
being sent home. But I also knew there was more. A darker
hurt ate at me. I felt for those I left behind. I always had them
on my mind and felt no one cared for them. I knew that their
families did. Did their country? Did the ones who were
responsible for letting Vietnam go on for so long? Someone
had to be their voice. We owed something to them.

It angered me every time I remembered a friend who died.
I'd see his young face and remember the laughing and joking
around. I'd remember the pain and the crying, especially
Williams, Bunting, Orgeron, and Washington. They were in
my platoon. There were others too, ones in the company, the

brave men of company "A," 2nd Battalion, 60th Infantry, 9th Division.

I found myself looking for old letters. My Army duffle bag in the garage had some military orders and about a hundred letters. The hall closet had boxes of letters. Most of them were either from my wife or to her, but there were others, too, from other vets and friends who had written me while I was over there.

I opened one from my mother and started to cry. My throat got a lump. No one was home. I could cry if I wanted to, but why now?

My mother had only been thirty-eight when I was drafted. I can't imagine how it must have felt for her, having her child forced to fight a war. I envisioned my teenage daughter slinging a rifle and pointing it at gooks.

I folded the letter back up and stuffed it in the bag. The pain was too much.

But I couldn't keep stuffing my emotions. The letters would be a start. I decided to take notes from them and begin a journal. I've always been a guy who had to keep things in order.

My barely-controlled anger worried me, but what worried me more was the thought that I might never be able to change. Was there a cure for this PTSD? Although I felt I was finding some answers, there were so many more left to go.

Did Joe have a few pieces of the puzzle for me? Maybe, but I feared far more of the pieces had been left back in some rice paddy, rubber plantation, or in one of the other messed-up places I had been privileged to visit while on duty in southeast Asia. The Animals' "We've Got To Get Out Of This Place" had been one of the most popular songs in Vietnam. Twenty years later I still felt like I had never left.

Chapter Four

"DAD, THE PHONE! It's Sandy, long distance!" my daughter Michelle shouted.

I grabbed the phone. Sandy and I had met when we were loading buses at the Red Cross Station back in '69. We were being sent to the Army induction center in Jacksonville and from there to Fort Benning, Georgia for basic training. A few of us from Clearwater actually made it through basic, Army infantry training (A.I.T.) and even Vietnam together—Sandy, Dave, Dan, Harvey, and myself. As Sandy and I chatted about the mundane stuff, I found myself thinking back to those early days we had shared.

✪ ✪ ✪

IT WAS SEPTEMBER of '69 when a young group of boys from Clearwater, Florida arrived to Fort Benning, Georgia. We were all uneasy about getting drafted. We stuck together as much as possible to keep each others spirits up. Sandy and I matched up right a way. He had a smart-aleck way about him that often caught the drill sergeant's attention. This of course didn't help me in the least.

For a few days we hung around a wooden barracks on the edge of the compound, which was the introduction station. From there we were supposed to be assigned to our basic training unit. Somehow they forgot about us, and we weren't about to call attention to ourselves. We'd sleep in late and then sneak off to the mess hall to eat and hurry back. We'd use the pay phones to call home a couple times a day—totally against the rules.

Then our luck ran out. We were all sleeping in late one morning when large black drill sergeant walked into the barracks and started bellowing at us.

"What the hell do you call this?" he shouted.

We all jumped out of bed.

Except Sandy.

"Damn...quiet man. I'm trying to sleep," he said.

I busted a gut.

The sergeant focused in on me with dark, mirthless eyes. "What's so funny, troop?" he asked.

"Nothing I guess. I just like to laugh," I said.

"Is that so? What's your name, boy?"

"Phil."

"Phil WHAT?" he blasted back at me.

"FERRAZANO," I shouted back.

"Who the hell is this ass in bed?"

He pivoted and strode over to Sandy's bunk. He flipped over the mattress with Sandy on it.

"Who in the hell do you think you are boy?" he asked Sandy.

"Damn, that's no way to wake a guy. Can't you talk a little a softer? What is it, ten o'clock? Some people need their sleep."

"You have got to be shitting me! Get your ass up and stand on that line on the floor! All of you stand at attention. NOW!"

We all jumped to the line and stood quiet at attention.

Sandy was making faces and kept on talking to me. I stood still trying not to laugh.

The sergeant jumped back and forth like a chicken with his head cut off. He picked his targets—Sandy and me.

"So Mr. Ferra-whatever-ya-name."

"Ferrazano, sir."

"God dammit it man, I'm not a sir! I work in this man's Army! I'm a drill sergeant. My name is Martin and I probably will have my number twelve straight up your ass before the eight weeks is up! So Mr. Ferri-lan-zio! You friends with this character?" He threw Sandy a scowl.

"I know him. And my name is Ferrazano."

"Is that so? What is it, I-Tal-ion or something?"

"Yes," I said.

"Yes what?"

"Yes it's Italian."

"God damn boy you dense! You answer, 'Yes DRILL SERGEANT!'" he blasted.

"Geez, this guy is gonna have a damn heart attack," Sandy mumbled.

The drill sergeant jumped within two inches of his face. He stared Sandy in the eye and gritted his teeth.

"You a damn hippy? You one of them longhaired wise guys? What's your last name?"

"Braun," said Sandy.

"What's that?" asked the sergeant.

"Braun, sir," replied Sandy.

"GOD DAMN! YOU AS DUMB AS YA BUDDY!"

"What? You asked me my name and I told you."

"What nationality are you boy. Think hard now. You sure the hell ain't no African American. You ain't smart enough for that!"

"I'm Jewish."

"You have got to be shitting me! They send me an Italian and a Jew together this time. I can't handle that! But dammit I will try. I'll work both your sorry asses! You'd better hope you get into my platoon. Oh yeah, boys. I'll make you fightin' men. You wanna be fightin' men?"

He looked at Sandy for an answer.

"Well, no not really. I was drafted. Hell, I'd rather be

racing my car back home."

"That ain't the right answer boy!" shouted the sergeant.

That day we were assigned to details all over the camp. I was on KP at least twice—a double shift. Long days from four in the morning until late into the evening. We still had civilian clothes and penny loafer shoes. Others had already been issued boots and fatigues. We seemed out of place.

Late one evening we were mopping the floors. Hot water was being thrown all over. One big pot splashed the tops of my shoes and burned my feet.

I let out a scream and threw the mop. I stormed out of the mess hall. When I got outside I just kept on walking until I was just outside the gate. I'd leave. They couldn't keep me here. My mind was set to do it when I heard a soft voice.

"Where the hell you think you're going, son?"

I turned and saw a shadow with a Smokey-the-Bear hat, sitting on a picnic table. As he walked towards me I realized who it was: Drill Sergeant Martin.

"Man, they burned my feet. It's bullshit. I've had damn KP for three straight days. Bullshit, man."

"It is son, and that's what it's gonna be for the next eight weeks."

The sergeant was talking soft and not screaming. I wasn't use to that.

"Look, you get back to your barracks. Go back to the mess hall first and tell the guy in charge I said for you to go and get some sleep. Just tell him Martin said so. He'll let you go."

"Thanks."

"That's okay. See, I can be as gentle as a lamb but don't fuck with me. If ya get into my platoon you'll be flying right. I have the best damn platoon here. I'm at Sandhill. So if you get assigned there, odds are I'll be your drill instructor."

"Okay, Drill Sergeant."

"See, ya already learning. And that fuck-head buddy of

yours better learn too. Clue him in. I don't take any shit from
no damn hippy." I felt better that Martin was talking to me as a
human being now. I figured it was all part of the game.

We were up at the crack of dawn, awakened by the reveille
trumpet that sounded throughout the Georgia pines. The
mornings were cold and damp, always foggy with the scent of
the pine trees in the air. It reminded me of Christmas but
without presents. We were now issued fatigues, boots and hats.
We were on our way to being whatever they could make of us.
I had my doubts about being a fighting man. None of us looked
anything like a soldier.

The buses pulled up to where we were lined up at
attention. The bus that was in front of us stopped short and the
door flung open. As it did, a tall, slender, drill sergeant
appeared. He cocked his head back and grinned. It was Martin.
I felt at ease, figuring he was a nice guy. Wrong. In a second he
darted off the bus screaming like a wild man, screaming at each
of us to get on the bus, yelling at the top of his lungs because
we couldn't get on the bus fast enough.

"You made it!" he yelled.

No one said a word but Drill Sergeant Martin.

"Yes sir, you all in my platoon! The third and best damn
platoon here at Sandhill, Fort Benning Georgia. You gonna
make ya mama proud! Ain't that right Mr. Braun?"

"If you say so," answered Sandy.

I hoped Sandy would stop the smartass talk, but it just
wasn't in him. He wasn't mean; it was just that the drill
sergeant was perfect fodder for Sandy's wisecracks.

"You gonna be a hard one, ain't ya, boy?" Martin said.

Sandy decided to stay quiet for the time being. We all did,
but Martin kept on us every chance he got. He had a job and he
did it well. He was Army and he was a 'Nam vet. We learned
to respect him and when it got down to it, he would be there for
us.

I grinned as I thought about basic with Sandy, Martin and the others. Here it was years later and I was still having to deal with my service experience.

✪ ✪ ✪

"WHEN YOU COMING up?" Sandy asked, bringing me back to the present. He always wanted me to come see him in Tennessee. A few years ago he had decided to quit the service station business he owned in Clearwater and move up north. He had a new job with a company that did construction for insurance claims.

I'd made a couple of trips, and loved the scenery. Getting into the mountains might clear my head.

"How you feeling? Getting any help from the VA?" he asked.

I told him about the Vet Center and the PTSD.

"I knew that a long time ago. They just figured it out?"

"I see a counselor every week and I might go into the hospital for a stress program," I said.

"You should take Dan with you. He needed help even before he left the Army," Sandy said.

Dan was another buddy from Clearwater that had been drafted into Vietnam with us.

"I've talked to him about it. He won't go. He's a mess; at times it scares the hell out of me," I said. "Remember in A.I.T. when he went off and got wasted and then came back and punched out the mirrors in the latrine? He was so pissed about getting drafted. Then he does twelve months on the line and is afraid to return home to the States. The war did a number on him," I said.

✪ ✪ ✪

I REMEMBERED AN INCIDENT while on bunker watch in Tan An. I was assigned to bunker security in our headquarters company after I was wounded—not a bad job. I never complained because I knew I'd be sucking mud again in the bush. It was bad enough catching sniper fire and a few mortars now and then, but believe me, nothing compared to what I had been through.

I was sitting on the top level of my two-story lookout bunker when I happened to glance over to the chopper pad less then a hundred yards away. I saw this short guy dragging and kicking a wounded Viet Cong. The VC was taller than the GI.

Dan? I wondered.

The figure was heading to the POW tent in back of my bunker.

"Hey Danny!" I yelled. I hadn't seen him since we were separated when we first got in country.

"Phil? Is that you?" he shouted.

"Yeah, Dan. It's me. What the heck you doing here?" I shouted back.

"I thought you were a dead man," he said as he gave his disoriented prisoner a shove into the tent. "There you go, you little shit," he mumbled at the VC. "You'd better be glad I didn't cut off your ears."

Dan walked over to my bunker and I quickly made my way down from the upper level.

"You're all right," he said, clapping me on the back. "I didn't hear anything about you after the attack in Cambodia."

"You want a beer?" I asked, not wanting to think of Cambodia.

"Hell yeah man—what do you think?"

Dan had a real nervous look about him. Not uncommon for a guy always in the bush. He was worn out. He had changed into a hardcore warrior, a survivalist.

He had hated the Army and being drafted, like I had and

still did. But Dan was different now. He was used to the war and loved the excitement. It bothered me to see my buddy transformed into a seasoned soldier.

"When you guys got hit I heard the whole thing over the radio," he said. "We weren't far from you. They were pounding you guys pretty bad."

"Yeah no kidding. It was unbelievable, I'm one lucky guy. Someone was watching over me."

"Yeah I hear ya," he said as he downed a cold one. He grabbed another, popped it open with a church key and chugged it. "Man, I needed that." He wiped his mouth with the back of his hand. "The next day the group that hit you hit us. They kicked our butts, buddy," he said as he closed his eyes, threw back his head, and took another gulp.

We all should have been better prepared to fight against the well-trained hardcore NVA. In the delta with the 9th we had mainly been up against booby traps and small groups of Viet Cong. They hit and ran. That was bad enough.

They'd smile at you has they worked in the rice paddies, and then at night the little shits would set their deadly traps. You couldn't trust anyone.

I told Dan how I wound up in Tan An and how I was wounded.

"Why didn't they send your ass home?" he asked.

"No such luck." My voice rose. "Those bastards—they told me they would." I grabbed a beer. "Don't mean nothing, man. Who cares?"

I had been very bitter when I returned to my unit. If I couldn't be with my buddies in the field, then the hell with it. Send me home. What good was I anymore? I already felt like I didn't fit in.

As time went on, I realized my ass was best on the bunker line. I did my thing, even though I didn't get any recognition for it. Didn't matter. I already had my Combat Infantryman

Badge (CIB) and Purple Heart; nobody could change that.

Dan and I continued to drink and catch up on old times. Redman took guard so I could have some time with Dan. We walked around the base before he had to catch another chopper back to his company.

We hardly talked as we made our way to the chopper pad. I felt sorry for Dan knowing he had to return to the bush. I prayed this wouldn't be the last time I saw him.

"Dave is off line," Dan said. "I don't know what happened."

"What the hell will House Cat do without us?" I joked. House Cat was Dave's nickname. A shy kid with sad eyes, he had followed us around like a feline looking for a saucer of milk.

"Don't know, Phil. The guy was getting pretty messed up last time I saw him."

"I hate to hear that. He was so damn nervous on the plane coming over."

"Ol' House Cat... At least he's off line somewhere, I think," Dan said.

"Yeah, and Harvey and Sandy are off line now too. You're the only one still out there," I said. Harvey was in an engineer company somewhere. He had been separated from us as soon as we got over. Sandy was stationed at Fort Hood, Texas because of flat feet.

"No shit? I'd rather be in the bush. I belong now. They got what they wanted." Dan giggled as he chugged his last swallow. He bent the can and threw it hard in the direction of the chopper.

Dan couldn't stand still. His feet and hands constantly moved and jittered. His steel blue Paul Newman eyes moved in all directions. I watched him but didn't recognize the man I left only six months earlier.

I waved goodbye to Dan as he flew off on the slick. As it

banked, he smiled and waved, as did the door gunner. Dan looked sad. He had the look of those who had been leaving country the day we arrived. He had faced death, but so did I. Perhaps we both had the look.

I prayed to God as the chopper headed off. Just taking another weary grunt to another screwed up place—a mud hole, the Plain of Reeds, the border. It didn't matter. You weren't safe anywhere in that war-torn country.

I headed back to Redman in the bunker. Night came fast. I was back on and Redman went downstairs for some sleep. I knew he'd be back later. He always was. We kept each other company, even if it wasn't our turn for guard.

Alone, I listened to a little transistor radio and softly fingered an old guitar I had carried around for months. Bunny had given it to me, and it was the only part of him I had left.

As I'd quietly strummed, I'd think of this hero no one knew—but I knew, and that's what mattered.

Strains of "He Ain't Heavy, He's My Brother" crackled on the transistor radio. The words felt right as I thought of the guitar and the day I had with Dan and my dead friend who gave me the guitar I held.

As I listened I could still see Dan waving from the chopper. My thoughts drifted to the field and my platoon— Bill, Jerry, Dale, Phil, Ski, Wolf, Vic, and the others—still in Cambodia. I could still see the faces. It was hard to remember all the names, but the faces were hard to forget.

I couldn't recall one face and it got to me. Why couldn't I remember? I drew a blank. "Damn! It's his guitar and I can't remember his face," I muttered.

I stared off into the darkness. Only me and the song, "It's a long, long road" was part of the lyrics. "It sure is," I whispered.

"Wake up, you damn Army screw-up!" Redman shouted.

I snapped out of my thoughts.

"Hey Redman, how's it be?" I said, talking with a little GI

slang.

"Same, same, number one GI." Redman's eyes were red as hell. He had either smoked too much Cambodian red, or it was the beer. Probably a little of both.

"Will you stay awake with me?" I asked.

"Sure. I'll sit here and try to catch some sleep."

"I've got a better idea," I said. "How about you break into the mess hall and steal some of the colonel's ice cream?" The mess hall was only yards a few yards away from our lookout bunker. It reminded me of a building from the back lot of some John Wayne western—weathered clapboard siding and screens on the openings where windows should have been.

"Are you crazy?" Redman sputtered.

"Hell yeah! What the hell they gonna do? Draft us and send us to Viet-fucking-nam?"

"Got that right!" Redman said, laughing. "Be back in a few."

Redman left and minutes later we were gleefully eating some lifer's ice cream.

With the ice cream and the malaria pill I took earlier that day, I had to make a hasty retreat to the latrine. Not a good idea at night. Stories of guys getting blown away while using the latrine always worried me. I also had the thought of one of those big ass rats taking a bite out of my you-know-what, right before R&R.

Returning to the bunker, I found Redman doing a radio check. "How you read me? Over."

"Lima Charlie, bunker four."

"Roger that, out."

"Dumb REMF," Redman said after he hung up. REMFs stood for Rear Echelon Mother Fuckers. "Ain't this some shit man?"

"What?"

"Some of these mother fuckers have never been in the

bush."

"Yeah, who cares? Wish we were as lucky."

Redman agreed. His eyes drooped.

"Hey Redman, wake up. You're on guard."

"Fuck you. I just stole the old man's ice cream for you," he replied with eyes half-open.

"Yeah and I got the shits, me and my big ideas. Call over to Chris. See what he's doing."

"Bunker four, this is three, over."

"Hey man, what's up?"

"See anything?"

"Just a few rats in the wire, that's all."

"Blow the little fuckers for some excitement," Redman said.

"Yeah, wake this place up," I said.

A claymore went off. The whole place went on alert.

"No sweat, this is bunker four. Thought I had a gook in the wire," Chris said.

We were laughing out of our minds. Chris was on the horn trying to act serious. He got off guard and made his way over to us.

"You're crazy man," I said.

"Yeah man, but not as crazy as you two," Chris said.

If we didn't have each other in Vietnam we would have really gone nuts.

✪ ✪ ✪

NOW I NEEDED MY comrades, my friends, even more.

Between the phone calls from friends, the Vet Center, and reading old letters, my mind was constantly back in 'Nam. I started to wonder about the others—Three-Six, where the hell was he? I never returned his letters that he wrote me while I still was in 'Nam.

"Heard you were hit, the day after me. If there is anything I can ever do for, you let me know," he wrote.

I pictured him in my head looking at me with that damn bullet on the side of his nose. My lips tightened. I was pissed. The whole thing could have been avoided; we could have done it differently.

I wondered if Three-Six still thought about that day as I did, a movie replaying on eternal loop.

"The letter. He sent me a letter. I've got to find it," I mumbled.

I searched through closets, old boxes, everywhere. I remembered my duffle bag stuffed away under a workbench in the garage that I had found just the other day. I dumped it out on the concrete floor. I found more letters and old papers I had in Vietnam, mostly hospital records and traveling orders. I was sorting things out like I was hunting for some lost treasure. I felt I was piecing my life together. I wanted something back that I'd lost along the way. I wish I knew what it was.

I found a Western Union telegram.

"Your husband was wounded to the head while on a night time ambush in Cambodia."

That was it. No condition, no nothing.

Man! My poor wife and family. The words on the telegram were much too cold.

I was worth more than just a couple of lines.

I cried, and again I found myself alone.

Chapter Five

ALTHOUGH I LOOKED FORWARD to my meetings with Joe at the Vet Center, I didn't feel comfortable telling people I was being counseled. It was hard to admit that I still had underlying issues relating to 'Nam.

When I first returned home from Vietnam in 1971, people were already tired of hearing about the war. Most veterans locked their emotions away.

At our next session, Joe dispatched with the niceties. "Phil, you look wired," he said, his forehead wrinkling.

"I've been looking through old letters. They upset me. And I need a resolution on my claim. I'm not working now. It's hard."

Joe nodded. He pushed his glasses back on his nose, swiveled his chair toward his desk, and started to take notes.

"Okay, last week you were quite upset when you told me about your lieutenant getting shot. Some story."

"A nightmare," I said.

"So you got him out of there, right?"

I sighed and took a deep breath.

"Yeah, after about three tries with the chopper."

I STARTED MY JOURNEY back to the event. It didn't take long. It seemed the ordeal was eternally on my mind.

After we finally got Three-Six onto a chopper, I collapsed, exhausted and traumatized.

The platoon checked the place out and examined the dead NVA soldiers. I didn't help. I remembered the enemy's eyes as we took aim at them.

If I killed any, I really didn't want to know. I didn't want the image of a dead man I might have killed staying in my mind.

✪ ✪ ✪

"I HAVE TO GO to the bathroom, Joe." I just needed a breather already. My heart was racing and I couldn't control the volume of my voice.

"Sure, take your time."

I opened the door and headed off to the restroom, passing a work study doing his homework at the front desk, waiting for the phone to ring.

Maybe we'll be done, I thought as I washed my hands in the restroom. I looked in the mirror. Horrible. My eyes were bloodshot. In my mind I was a twenty-year-old, but the mirror didn't lie. I was middle-aged, faced with Vietnam trauma again.

I cursed myself for letting my emotions get the best of me. I felt as if I didn't know who I was anymore. Had I left the real me back in the jungle? Will the real me, the ass-hole, please stand up?

I dried my hands and shook my head. "Man I'm losing it," I said to the mirror.

When I returned to Joe's office, he was on the phone with another vet in trouble.

"I'll see you tomorrow," he said into the receiver. "Hang in there."

"Well are you ready?" He hung up the phone and turned his chair back toward me.

I nodded and took a deep breath.

"Wait," Joe said, getting up to tell the work study guy to hold his calls until we were done.

"Okay," he said, settling back into his chair. "So Three-Six is gone, the NVA is gone, and now what?"

"Sergeant Washington took over," I said. "Sergeant Williams had been assigned to another platoon when we went into Cambodia. He had always been there for me, broke me in the way I was breaking in Bunny."

"Bunny...the guy who laid down fire for the medic, right?"

"Right." I paused again, feeling the tears well up in my eyes. I never realized how much thinking of Bunny hurt.

✪ ✪ ✪

WE HEADED BACK to catch up with the rest of the company. As we left the area, thunder started and the sky became gloomy. A light rain trickled, giving the jungle a strange glow. No one spoke. Event the jungle grew silent.

Soon darkness slid into the jungle. Our plans were to form a large perimeter with the rest of the company. Usually we'd do this with a single platoon, but setting up something of this scale meant the captain was suspecting something. Something bad.

Once we joined up with the company, everyone dug in for the night. Sergeant Washington and I had to meet with the captain and go over the details of what had happened.

"Fine job you men did today," boasted our weary captain.

Fatigue hung on him, and his forehead furrowed. It was the first time I'd ever seen him worried. This was not a good sign.

"Hope Three-Six will be all right," I said. "He took a round right to the head."

"You all right?" Sergeant Washington asked. "This Cambodia stuff has already been hell on you."

"I can't wait till we get this mission over with. How long you think we gotta stay here?" I asked.

They both just shook their heads.

By the time we made it back to our section it was dark so we just lay down between Bill's foxhole and Bunny's, each about ten feet on either side of us.

Jerry and a couple others went out on LP. They set up their listening post fifty yards out and lay down in a grass hut they found.

"How you reading me?" I called in to Jerry.

"Lima charlie, you shithead." Lima charlie meant "loud and clear."

"That's affirmative," I replied back.

Jerry had been the battalion RTO before me. I made RTO right before we were ordered into Cambodia.

"You were in a bad situation with Three-Six," said Washington.

"Roger that, Sarge. I'm still shaking," I said.

"I'm gonna put you, Three-Six, and Doc in for Bronze Stars. You saved the lieutenant's ass."

"I hope I did. He didn't look good, though." We talked, but Washington started to nod off. I was wide awake when Bunny crawled over to my position.

"What the hell you doing, you little shit?" I asked Bunny.

"How did I do today?" he asked.

"If it wasn't for you, Doc could never have made it to me."

Bunny lit up like a Christmas tree. He grinned from ear to ear. Before this he was always the FNG, the fucking new guy. Nobody got close to him except me. Williams had looked after me and now I looked after Bunny.

"Do you like the guitar?" he asked.

The month before, our whole company area was burned to the ground. We lost everything.

I had a guitar that was with the 9th Division ever since the early years of the war. It was passed down to me. If the 9th Division got to go home, then I would be able to keep the guitar. It had names of guys who served in Vietnam from all different years. When the guitar burned up, a piece of each guy went up in smoke.

Bunny had bought me a replacement at the PX and had presented it to me with a flourish.

I smiled at Bunny and said, "Look buddy, when we get back to our base camp in Tan Tru I'll teach you some chords. It's our guitar."

"Thanks, Phil."

"Yeah, and thanks for helping me, buddy," I said.

Bunny was a hero to me. He knew I was in trouble and did what he could. He was part of us. He broke his cherry. No more FNG, no more fucking new guy. It was the happiest I'd ever seen him.

Bunny crawled back to his foxhole. He was sitting up and I could see his steel pot in the dim moonlight. The rain was still light, but harder than that afternoon. We tried to get comfortable under the one poncho we were sharing.

"Ain't this a bitch man?" I said.

"What?" Washington said, rolling back over to face me.

"All the money being spent on this war and we have to share a poncho."

"Yeah. Why did I come back for a second tour? I'm nuts," the sergeant said.

I thought the same thing, but didn't want to tick him off. Then again, how could anyone get more ticked than he already was—shot at all stinking day, lying in mud, hungry as hell. We both were.

"Hey, Sarge," I said.

"What, Fernandez?"

"You must be one stupid lifer."

We both laughed. I really didn't know him well—none of

us did. I thought he was anxious to see combat, until we walked into the NVA camp that day.

"And it's Ferrazano, not Fernandez," I added.

"Sorry 'bout that."

"Used to it. They always change me from Italian to Spanish."

"Can't screw up 'Washington,'" he said, grinning.

I talked with him most of the night. He was an all-right guy. He was just doing his job and trying to have a career. He wanted a good life for his wife and kids.

"You E4?" asked Washington.

"Yeah, right. I'm still PFC and carrying the battalion radio. Ain't that against some Army code or something?" I chuckled.

Usually it was a sure thing to become an E-5 sergeant when you carried the higher radio. The job carried a lot of responsibility.

"You'll make it. Don't worry," said Washington.

I didn't care about rank, but once I got back to the world I could have lived off base, and the extra money would have helped. I never gave it much thought; I just wanted out in one piece with my head screwed on straight. I saw a lot of guys go nuts from the hellhole. I knew guys who shot each other in the feet to get out of the bush. It didn't sound like a bad idea at times.

The radio crackled. "We're hearing movement. Over," reported Jerry.

"Yeah, what's up? Over," I answered.

"There's movement, maybe setting up mortar tubes. I don't know."

"Maybe tigers. Can't do anything. Just keep awake and call me back soon," I said.

"Roger that. Out." Jerry replied with a whisper.

Jerry and I were good friends and I started to worry. He

was going through a rough time. Only a few days before we left for Cambodia he had been handed a "Dear John" letter from the chaplain. I could tell it really upset him.

He called back. "Look, we're crawling out of this hut. There's a fallen tree, a big one. We'll get under it."

"Roger that," I said.

It was a good idea to get out of the grass hut—a lot more protection under the fallen tree if the lead and shrapnel started to fly. Jerry and the two old-timers with him knew what they were doing, probably better than most.

I let my guard down and so did Washington. We should have dug in. We screwed up. Being too tired was no excuse. Who would have anticipated what was about to occur? I couldn't imagine anything worse than what I had just experienced only a few hours earlier with Three-Six.

"You know I have four kids," Washington said, half-dozing. "I love 'em." It was almost as if he was talking in his sleep.

"Yeah, I'm sure they love you too."

"Let me get on your side," he said.

I didn't know why he wanted to change positions. We rolled over each other, as if we were doing a figure eight football drill, minus one guy. Washington turned away from me and fell asleep.

I wasn't so lucky. I had to take the situation reports or sit-reps every half hour. In between I tossed and turned, trying to get some rest.

It was almost four-thirty in the morning and I hadn't gotten any sleep as usual. I rested by just closing my eyes. I wanted to sleep badly. I needed it, but knew I'd be awakened by the radio. Falling asleep in between sit-reps made me feel as though I had a hangover.

I slept only when I knew I wouldn't be interrupted. Like when there was a three-day stand down, no duty. I'd get wasted

and drink until I passed out. I forgot everything then. That was
the way to sleep.

✪ ✪ ✪

"HOW THE HELL could anyone sleep with that kind of shit
going on?" I blasted out.

"That angers you, doesn't it?" Joe said.

"Yeah, living like a damn animal gets me mad as hell. No
reason for it."

I sat there and tried to collect my thoughts again. "How do
you listen to these stories all the time, Joe?"

"At times it gets rough. Then I need a time out. I get out of
Dodge."

I shook my head. I couldn't do what he did each day. You
had to be a strong person to deal with everyone else's
memories of Vietnam.

✪ ✪ ✪

IT WAS ALMOST four-thirty and there wasn't a single sound.
I felt I was the only one of sixty men who was awake. I knew
that wasn't true, but I still felt alone. Our screwed up day
haunted me, and I couldn't stop thinking about Three-Six.

The LP hadn't called in for over a half hour. I figured they
were having a rough time staying awake so I called them.

"Commo check," I said low, and then hit the button on the
handset a few times in case they were sleeping. The crackling
sound it made echoed throughout the jungle.

"Yeah, I hear ya. Nothing. Out," answered a sleepy voice.

Maybe I can catch some real sleep for a few minutes, I
thought. *Hell, everyone else was sleeping.*

I rolled over.

BOOM!

We were hit. Washington and I took the first mortar round. We didn't even hear it whistling in. I was hit to the back of the head, the back, and right shoulder. I rolled back over.

"Oh God," were my first words. I placed my fingers to my head. Warm blood dripped down my arm. My head must have been wide open. I couldn't move my left arm; red-hot shrapnel burned into my back. I reached for Washington.

"Come on!" I yelled, trying to pull him to Bill's foxhole. I pulled him over, almost on top of me.

His eyes were closed. Blood and muscle hung out of his neck and on top of his shoulder.

I yelled at him again. He gave one moan. I knew he was dead. I had my arm over him to protect him from the mortars that were starting to pound us one by one.

BOOM! BOOM!

A steady bombardment. Round after round, each hit another scream. Screaming of young men in agony. That's what's hard to forget. That deep, terrible scream I'd never heard before. The scream of death.

"YOU OKAY?" JOE asked, reaching to comfort me.

His eyes were telling me he heard the horror before. He knew I hurt—a hurt he knew I've been carrying around for a long time.

THEY WERE HOLDING Bill down in his foxhole, but he was trying to get to me. No one could get out of the holes. It looked like the Fourth of July at the finale of a huge fire works display.

The horrifying *clang clang clang* of a machine gun was

directly on us.

I could hear the trees being cut up. Our men were popping claymore mines. A new guy on LP in another platoon panicked, stood up, and ran in. Friendly fire cut him down.

I looked over to Bunny. I only saw his upper body sitting up, no steel pot. No head to go in it, either.

"Oh, my God!" I screamed out in panic. "Bunny, Bunny!" But I knew my buddy was dead.

I thought I was next.

"No!" I yelled.

In a panic I took my M-16 and sprayed right over Bill's foxhole. I could see green traces coming in my direction.

"Don't get up!" I yelled to Bill. I franticly fired on full automatic over the tops of their heads.

"Don't shoot," yelled the captain, not wanting us to give away our positions.

Damn it, man! I thought. *They already had our positions.*

I just lay there thinking it would never end. Mortars still landed all around. When would it stop?

If I die then I won't have to hear it anymore and then I can get some sleep, I thought.

The ringing in my ears was so loud it almost muffled the blasts, but the ground jolted with every impact. Each hit took a piece of my heart—a heart much older now than the twenty years it had been on this earth.

Can't even buy a drink back in the world yet, I thought.

"No! I ain't dying in this hell hole!" I screamed. "Oh Lord, please," I cried.

I could see my new wife looking over me. I could see her beautiful blue eyes, her long brown hair, her kind smile. A warm sensation spread throughout my body. I was not afraid to die. It was okay. If it was meant to be, then so be it. I was getting weaker. "I'm sorry honey, I'm sorry," I said.

After what seemed like ages, Jerry and Doc knelt over me.

"You'll make it buddy," Jerry said. "You'll be drinking milkshakes with your wife before you know it." His deep southern drawl comforted me. I wasn't alone.

Doc Izard gave me a shot of morphine in the thigh to calm me down. "He's hit in the head and back," I heard Doc tell Jerry through the drugged haze.

"How bad?"

"Don't know man. Doesn't look good."

"Hang in there, buddy," Jerry said. His voice cracked as he put his hand on me.

As the son rose, the jungle floor was littered with young men in pain. Doc ran from wounded man to wounded man, nervously tending to all those he could.

The NVA broke. We were out of artillery reach and it took a while for the choppers to start coming in to get us out. What took maybe twenty or thirty minutes of getting the shit kicked out of us seemed like forever.

Being the first position hit made the nightmare worse. Wounded and helpless, I couldn't find cover. All I could do was watch others getting wounded.

Finally they loaded me into a chopper with about twenty others. I lay on the warm metal floor of the chopper, silent. The sounds of others were too overwhelming for me to think about my own pain. Guts hung out of one. He held them in his hands, laughing and babbling.

"I'm going home!" he shrieked.

The scout dog had been hit. His trainer threw him on the chopper.

"Sorry, man," the door gunner yelled through the thumping of the chopper blades whirling in the darkness. "There's no room for the dog."

The dog, his sides heaving and soaked with blood, was put off for more room for the wounded...and the dead.

There were too many. One was too many. One more life

lost for this miserable war was just too much to ask.

It was over, at least for me. As we took off, I watched my guys waving at me. In a short time I'd seen them age. The clothes were rotting off their backs. The dirty faces and the blood—was it over? Had I done enough to have the right to go home while others were left to continue with the war?

It didn't matter to me that most in 'Nam were not involved in actual combat. I was a grunt and I identified with those brave men who had. We combat soldiers didn't fight for the government or our officers. We fought for each other, so we could all make it home. That's what it was all about.

Chapter Six

AS DAY BROKE, I remember traveling fast and high as the choppers banked toward the hospital in Tay Ninh back in Vietnam. A new day and a new beginning for me, or so I hoped. Although my condition was uncertain, I believed the war would be over for me, one way or another. The medivac choppers landed and quickly carried me and the other wounded off into Quonset huts, metal, half-circle shelters.

Seeing the buildings made me feel safe. The 93rd Evac Field Hospital reminded me of stateside duty.

I couldn't believe how many were wounded. The room was full—line after line of men crying and screaming. I didn't know if they were all from my company or from other ones. It was hard to recognize people covered with blood.

I wanted to cry, to raise my voice with the other wounded soldiers in the hospital. But I couldn't let myself. I knew I needed to be tough to survive.

Lieutenant Garcia lay next to me, screaming. It was hard to find even a square inch of his body that wasn't soaked with blood from the shrapnel that had dug into his body.

"Please knock him out," I whispered. "Please." I closed my eyes. I couldn't take it any longer.

A team of doctors approached me. "We have to operate on you, son," a masked doctor said.

I said nothing. The nurses ran from wounded to wounded taking care of the worst first.

"We're putting you to sleep," said the nurse as they rolled me into the operating room.

"I can dig that," I said.

She smiled.

I needed sleep. I wanted so much to be knocked out. Hearing the others was driving me crazy.

Before we entered the operating room, a doctor looked down at me. "What happened? Can you tell me?" he asked.

"They followed us during the day and hit us this morning with everything."

"It's all right now. The war is over for you."

I gave a half smile and closed my eyes. I realized he had just wanted to see how alert I was. I started to feel the effects of the IV inserted in my arm. After the nurse adjusted the flow in the lines, she squeezed my hand to comfort me. The mark it must have made on her life to witness young men, barely out of high school, fighting for their lives.

I counted backwards from one hundred. I reached ninety-five before I dropped into blackness.

I woke up hours later in a hallway. There was a Vietnamese nurse humming and cleaning the Cambodian red clay out from under my fingernails. I had the stuff embedded all over my body, deep into my skin. The clay gave soldiers an orange suntan, like if you had mixed a sunscreen of iodine and baby oil.

I tried to raise up on one elbow. The pain knocked me back down. I could feel the deep sensation of cut nerves and muscle in my back. My head throbbed through the bandage. Tight stitches over my left ear and along my neck pulled at my skin. My ears still rung loudly. My left arm was in a sling and my right arm ached with a piece of shrapnel left in my shoulder. Finally I gave in to the fatigue and dropped back to sleep.

When I stabilized, I was sent to the 24th Evac Hospital in Long Binh. From there I was told I'd either go to Japan or back to the States. Usually with a head wound you were out of there.

At least that's what I thought.

As soon as I could I wrote home. "Well honey, your little GI got himself wounded," my note said. "Don't worry. I'm all right. It looks like I might come home. A lot of doctors here are against the war and they like to send guys home."

I stayed in the hospital for about the next ten days waiting to be sent to Japan and then home.

"How do you feel?" asked a doctor, reading my chart. He wasn't one of the regular doctors. I had never seen him before.

"My head hurts. I hurt."

"I'm sending you back to your unit," he said. "Just stay away from loud noises and you'll be fine."

My jaw dropped. He had caught me off guard. I wondered if this guy was looking at the right chart.

He walked away without another word.

I lay there like a guy who had someone's thumb up his ass.

"Man, no way!" I said as the nurse walked by. "Is this doctor for real? I can't go back to Cambodia! That's where my company is."

"Go back to the base you have in 'Nam," she said, shaking her head disgusted in the wake of the doctor. "I thought you'd go home."

"Me too."

I had a little bag with some personal items, a new set of boots, and fresh fatigues. Oh yeah, and a Purple Heart medal. That was it.

Arm in a sling, bandage still around my head, ears ringing and a hole in my back about three inches by three inches that had to be cleaned every day, I walked out of the hospital.

I stood outside the hospital, not knowing were to go. It would be dark soon. A guy in a jeep pulled up next to me. "Where you going soldier? They're letting you out?" he asked.

"No shit!" I snapped. "I need a ride to Tan Tru."

"Look," he said, "I have to pick up a truck in the morning

and then I can take you there. I'll bring you to a place you can sleep for the night. Jump in."

I guess I was lucky to find this guy. He probably saw a lot of wounded guys leaving the hospital like me.

"Where were you hit?"

"Cambodia."

"Whoa, that was some heavy shit, I heard. The 25th caught a lot. Who were you with?"

"The 9th, attached to the 25th," I said, not wanting to talk about it.

He shook his head. "It must have sucked."

I looked at him and nodded. I was suffering with the biggest migraine headache I'd ever had. My stomach writhed. I pictured everyone home preparing for my homecoming while I was preparing to get my sorry ass shot at again.

Was this the way to treat a wounded soldier, a guy who had just experienced a lifetime of horror? Wasn't I worthy of being sent home? My wounds were not enough. My blood that spilled all over Cambodia didn't mean a thing.

I was now a changed man, hardened by war; my mind did a complete about face. I had been against the war right from the start but never doubted my military obligation. Not now.

What the hell were we fighting for? It was all wrong. All the dead and wounded for what? What the hell did a young kid know? Only what he was told, that's what. I didn't have time to form my own opinion about anything because they drafted my young ass right out of high school.

One day I'm cruising through Steak 'n Shake with my friend Wally in his big brown '55 Caddy looking for girls. The next I'm sucking mud, drenched in a rice paddy in the Mekong Delta. I'd heard about 'Nam since I was fourteen years old. I had enough time to weasel my sorry self out of being drafted. Guess I was too damn stupid.

I was thinking all these negative thoughts while the driver

watched the road. There was dust and dirt all over the place, and the ride down the highway was bumpy as hell. Each jolt surfaced more anger. I had bought a '67 Pontiac a few months before Uncle Sam sent me his greetings. I thought for sure I'd be back home cruising around in it in no time.

I had a letter in my pocket from the doctor that stated, "Protect from any loud noises." What a fucking joke. Where was I to go in Vietnam and stay away from loud noises? I didn't have a clue.

It was just about dark when we pulled up to a barracks made out of sandbags and ammo grates, an all too familiar sight. Not a soul anywhere.

"Look man, you hungry?" the driver asked. "Maybe I can find you something."

"No, my head is killing me. Where's the aid station?"

"I'll take you there."

"I need something for a bad headache," I said to the medic on duty. I explained I just got out of the hospital.

"Didn't they give you anything for pain?" he asked.

"No," I snapped in disgust.

The medic reached into a drawer and pulled out some aspirin.

I took four. "Can you clean my back in the morning before I leave?"

"Sure. Let me take a look."

I pulled out my shirt with one hand and the medic lifted my shirt.

"Why the hell didn't they sew you up?"

"Who the heck knows, man. Can it get infected?"

"Hell yes."

I shook my head.

"Stop by in the morning, I'll clean it and put a new bandage on. Keep an eye on it. You should have stitches."

We left and the driver took me back to the barracks.

"Look, no one's here. Find a bunk, get some sleep and I'll pick you up in the morning. We'll stop by and get that bandage changed before we leave, okay?"

"Thanks. Glad you came along."

He smiled and we shook hands.

I guess the driver must have been another guardian angel sent down to look over me. I was lucky in a way—at least I had made it out of Cambodia alive, but I feared the road ahead. Pain, fear, mistrust, and anger were to be my constant companions for my last eight months in 'Nam, and even further beyond.

I lay down and tried to sleep. I was very lonely in that empty barracks, a lost puppy away from his mother. But then I remembered God again. I thanked him for saving me. I wasn't mad that he couldn't get me out of Vietnam. I questioned him though—on a lot of things. Why? Why did the war go on for some and some didn't have to deal with it? I got no answer. I cried into my pillow.

Artillery guns fired in the night, shaking the barracks. They were right in back of the building and I didn't know it.

"My head! My head!" I screamed.

BOOM! BOOM! BOOM!

I tried to cover my ears from the noise. Nothing worked. My head felt like it was going to explode. I didn't know if I could handle it.

Morning finally came and the driver arrived with his truck to pick me up.

"Looks like you didn't sleep," he said.

"No shit—guns going off all night," I said.

We got into the dump truck and after another stop at the aid station to change my bandages, we headed off down the bumpy road. The driver kept the pedal floored as he went through the gears. The ride in the World War II vintage duce-and-a-half was worse then the ride in the jeep.

Out of nowhere, a Vietnamese farmer with a water buffalo crossed the road right in front of us. The driver slammed on the brakes and swerved, careening into a ditch.

I was jolted forward, then back hard against the seat. I felt as if my back was being branded with a hot poker. My wounds had opened up and I could feel it bleed again.

✪ ✪ ✪

"YOU BASTARDS!" I SCREAMED. Like never before, my anger spat at those who sent me to Vietnam.

Joe sat quietly, listening.

"This is hard, man. I'm so upset I can hardly breathe."

"You have a right to be upset," Joe said. "I would be too."

Just that single affirmation made me feel so much better. Someone was listening to me, after all these years. I wasn't crazy. Anybody treated like that would be mad. Joe had just said so.

"I can't go on, Joe. I have another headache," I said.

"We can talk next week," he said. "Look, if you need me, call. I'm concerned about you."

"Yeah, me too. I'll call if I need you."

"You should go to the stress recovery unit at the hospital. I already told them you might be coming in. Here's the number. You'll talk with a guy named Bob Roberts. He's a good man."

I left, stepping into the restroom. My head pounded and my shirt was drenched with sweat. I splashed cold water on my face and looked into the mirror.

I was still looking at a confused man, but this time it was a man who knew he had deep feelings about what he had done, and about what had happened to him in Vietnam. I knew I was angry about being ordered out of the hospital too early, but there had to be more to it than that.

At least now I knew that leaving the hospital probably

caused more pain than the wounds themselves. They misled me
into believing I was going home. They lied to me. I resented it,
and there was no way I could get even. I had been helpless
then, and I felt the same way now.

I also had the feeling things would get worse before they
got better. The calm before the storm, like it was in 'Nam. The
quiet of the jungle, right before an ambush. Could I handle the
stress of that again? I really didn't know.

Chapter Seven

MY IMMINENT HOSPITAL stay made me nervous. I'd be at the stress recovery unit, SRU, for two months and I didn't know what to expect or what type of guys I'd be living with.

Am I ready for this? I thought as I drove myself to the SRU. I needed to have tests done because of the pain. If it was the shrapnel, then it was giving me a signal. The pain was worse than it ever had been in the past. I hadn't been able to work for months. My anger bubbled close to the surface.

I flipped the radio on. Music had always been my escape, but it wasn't the same as when I was in high school and had enjoyed singing. "Somewhere Beyond the Sea" by Bobby Darin boomed out of the speakers. Now that guy could sing. I had always liked his music. It made me think back to when I was a kid in the early '60s when we just moved to Florida. I'd sit on the beautiful white sand beach and look out across the green waters of the gulf, thinking that maybe on a clear day I could actually see Mexico.

Singing along with the radio, I raised a smile and continued my twelve-mile drive to the hospital. Maybe there was peace in relating back into my youth. After all, the bastards cut it short. I was a happy kid with loving, hard-working parents, and a brother and two sisters. We fought like all siblings did, but defended each other to the end.

Was it my youth that I longed for? Maybe the past would hold a key to the future. The more I tried to analyze, the more confused I got.

I didn't need to find some other answer. It was 'Nam that

was screwing me up. I wasn't convinced that the hospital
would help. They already thought my pain was all in my head.
I knew I'd better keep my guard up. I saw the action and got
shot up. I deserved what they had to offer.

By the time I pulled into the hospital I was a basket case.

"Man, you've got to learn to calm down," I said to myself.
I tried to convince myself that maybe, just maybe, the hospital
might help. My head already hurt like hell and the day had just
begun. My worst headaches always seemed to be the ones that
woke me at around four in the morning. Sometimes they would
last for days. I was fed up with the years of suffering with
migraines.

I walked into hospital admissions at seven-thirty in the
morning on September 15, 1992. It made me think of when I
reported to basic training. That was in September 1969.

"I'm here for admission to SRU," I said to the nurse at the
counter. I walked past guys who were sitting around, some
looking sick, some pissed off. I knew the routine. I'd been in
their seats many times.

I felt privileged to be getting admitted, but it also pissed
me off. I had asked to be admitted before, always to be denied.
What was so different now?

I sat down and a nurse took my vital signs. "Do you have
high blood pressure?" she asked.

"I don't know," I said.

"It's a little high, and so is your pulse rate."

I knew that the reason my pressure was high was because
of the way I was ticking myself off. I knew it was one problem
I had; I'd think of all the crap I'd been through and it would eat
at me. My anger would cause my blood pressure to rise and I'd
get a headache. My ears would start to ring, my muscles would
tense and with all this, the pain would get worse.

The nurse directed me to the SRU building, located way in
back of the complex. Driving there in my truck, Credence

Clearwater Revival blasted out of the speakers. "Have you ever seen the rain? Coming down on a sunny day."

"In 'Nam it came pouring down all right," I said. I thought of the music again, how the tone of songs had changed during the war.

I sang in a top forties band as a teenager. Elvis was always one of my favorites, then The Beatles. Music exploded in my youth and every kid in the neighborhood had to have a guitar, but not all could sing. As I grew older I did a pretty good Elvis. I would learn the words—words of fun and young love.

Then came the words of horror, songs of protest—make love not war. I should have listened to the words. I learned the songs, but had I listened?

I grabbed my one suitcase and headed toward a loading dock where men were sitting around talking. One wore a baseball cap emblazoned with, "VIETNAM VET: We were winning when I left."

"Like your hat," I said, smiling.

"Where you headin'?"

"SRU."

He pointed down a hallway and directed me to the second floor. "SRU is on the left, and substance abuse on the right."

Oh man, I thought. *I don't want to be with a bunch of druggies.*

I trod the hall as if I was reporting to my next duty station. That uncertainty that had flooded my stomach at Sandhill, Fort Benning, Fort Puke—I mean Polk—and that place in Asia. It was all the same.

But maybe I could handle it better now. I had earned the right to be here. I approached the nurse's station anticipating some rude VA employee. It was the complete opposite; I was greeted with welcoming arms. I had made it to a mystical place. It was like I had been given the honor to be labeled a freakin' basket case. I had fought the 'Nam, so I could share the whole screwed nightmare with others who were worse than me, just so maybe I'd feel better.

"Mr. Roberts isn't here. He's on vacation so you'll have to meet with Jim Bedford. He'll explain the program to you," said the nurse. She showed me my room. I'd be sharing with nine other vets, but each bed had its own locker and privacy curtain.

"Everyone's off to lunch," she said. "You can put your things in your locker and then at one, go see Jim."

"Fine," I said. She left me with a smile and a handshake.

After I put my things in my locker, I headed down the hall. I peeked in the other rooms. They all looked the same.

In one room a guy sat reading. He looked up. "Hi, man. You new?" he asked, standing up and offering me his hand. He had jet black, long, unruly hair, dark eyes, and massive features. He reminded me of a bear.

"I'm Ed. I stay in here by myself because I snore like a damn motorboat. Less hassles. I don't want to bother anyone and I don't like for anyone to mess with me."

"I hear ya," I said. Not good to tick off this grizzly. "My name is Phil. Glad to meet you. I'm a little nervous about this hospital stay."

"Just don't listen to some of these guys. They all have stories. Form your own opinions, if you know what I mean," he said. "You a grunt?"

"Yeah, with the 9th. I got out of the field after I was wounded," I said.

"How bad were you hit?"

I told him, and he made me feel I belonged there.

At one, I walked into Bedford's office. A bearded man in his forties extended his hand. "Welcome," he said. His grip was firmer than his slight build would have led me to expect. "Excuse this mess. As you can see, I'm busy."

"Hi. I'm Phil."

"I know a little about you from Joe. Glad you're here."

Bedford explained the program and told me I would meet the head doctor, Dr. Camron, that afternoon.

"Don't be afraid to come see me if you need anything," he said. We shook hands again and I went out into the hallway.

"Hi, I'm Ed," said a heavy set man wearing a ball cap that read "Vietnam Vet And Proud Of It."

"Big Ed," another vet corrected.

Seemed the heavier of the two Eds, the one I had met earlier in the day, was Little Ed. Big Ed was a real comedian. I quickly discovered he could have the whole ward laughing in no time. Big Ed and I were to become good friends. We shared similar perspectives on 'Nam, and about life. Big Ed also faced health problems and PTSD. And he hid behind laughter—much like I did.

"When are you going in to see Dr. Camron?" asked Big Ed.

"Around three."

"He'll try to get to you."

"What to you mean?"

"You know, about 'Nam. To see if you're real or not."

Fuck. I was going to have to prove myself yet again to some medical asshole. My headache pounded. I wasn't in the mood for a damn head game.

"I don't give a damn what the hell he thinks. I know what I went through. This is bullshit!"

"Calm down, man. I didn't want to tick you off," said Big Ed with a chuckle.

"Touchy subject."

"You'll fit right in."

"I was afraid of that."

A voice boomed down the hall. "No damn way! Same fucking shit!" a thin, wiry guy yelled. He wore a Harley Davison t-shirt and had long hair and handlebar mustache. He pounded his fist on the reception desk and stormed past us, mumbling.

"Who pissed in his beer?" asked Ed.

The guy turned around and gave a half smile. "I'm just fed up with the VA shit. Name's Frank." We shook hands, and as with Ed, I became friends with Frank.

"I've gotta have a smoke. You wanna go outside and take a walk?" asked Frank.

"Sure," I said. We headed outside.

"You been here before?" I asked as he lit a cigarette, something I was glad I never did.

"Yeah, can you believe it?"

We walked away from the building and made our way to a dock that overlooked Tampa Bay. It was a nice quiet area away from the building. Not the same as the rest of the hospital. We walked past others standing around talking and smoking.

"I was in for twelve damn years and two tours of 'Nam," he said, taking a drag of his cigarette.

"No kidding." How could anyone handle two tours of 'Nam?

"I drank to hide the pain, and smoked some weed in the 'Nam. Good shit there. What about you?"

"Never smoked the stuff and I hardly drink. I've done my share of drinking in the past, though."

"Man you're unusual for being up here." He chuckled.

I told him about being wounded and my struggles and he did the same. Even though we looked like complete opposites, over time we learned to respect each other. The staff never understood our friendship, but we had a lot in common—both worked construction, had been married to the same woman for years, and became very uptight when talking about Vietnam. That's where we had the most in common—the 'Nam. One warrior can easily spot another.

"Gotta go. Have to see Camron," I said.

"Don't let him get under your skin."

"Don't worry. I won't."

"They've got their ways to push your buttons, dude."

"I'm not playing any games."

I headed upstairs for my appointment. I felt nervous, not because I'd be questioned about my tour and anything else he might come up with, but because of my anger. I knew I had a very short fuse and often looked for some asshole to tick me off. I didn't want to let loose, but if provoked, this doctor would see a side of me that most didn't—a side I tried hard to hide. I held in much hurt and anger. If I released it, it might be dangerous to me and anyone who got in my way. Joe knew this, and I had become more aware of it myself since I had been talking with him.

I walked into the doctor's small office located at the end of the hallway, next to Jim Bedford's. I glanced inside.

Bedford raised his head from his desk and asked, "Hi, Phil. You doing all right so far?"

"Yeah man, thanks. Gotta see Camron."

"He's in, go on in." I nodded and entered Dr. Camron's room. He stood up as I walked in and extended his hand. He was a thin man, mid-fifties, balding. He stared me down sternly.

"Hi, Phil. I'm Dr. Camron."

I felt at ease when I felt his firm handshake and the way he stared me down, stern, but direct. His eyes said, "I don't bullshit you, and you don't bullshit me." That's the way I liked it. No head games for me. This guy was going to listen to me, as did Joe, and I had to make him believe in me.

"Please take a seat. I want to ask you some questions."

I sat and took in a deep breath. *Here we go again,* I thought.

"I've read your folder and reports from Joe, and he feels you have PTSD along with health problems."

I started to explain the pain and the headaches. That was

my shield, a way for me to prove it wasn't all in my head. My
problems were more than PTSD.

"How was your childhood?"

"Great, I was a happy kid."

"Are your parents living?"

"Yes."

"Are they still married?"

"No, they were divorced a few years after I came back
from 'Nam."

"How old were you when this happened?"

"Around twenty-five."

"How old were you when you returned from 'Nam?"

"Twenty-one"

The questions continued and at times I felt like I was on
trial. It started to make me a feel uneasy. I knew what was
going on. He was trying to figure out if I had been fucked up
before the 'Nam.

"How long have you been married?"

"Twenty-three years."

He raised his eyebrows and said, "That's uncommon for a
guy with PTSD."

My temper started to kick in. My guard went up. I was
sick and tired of being questioned about what I had gone
through.

"So you must have been hurt when you were a little kid
and your parent's divorced?" he went on.

"I was twenty-five. It was four years after Vietnam."

"Oh yeah, that's right."

Now he was trying to mess with my mind, to trick me. His
smile didn't fool me.

Camron didn't know me yet and he didn't owe me a thing,
but the VA did for what the hell I'd been through.

I lost it.

"Look, man, all the shit I'm going through now is because

of 'Nam. That's it. I can't work. I hurt. I need medical care. What do you want to know? About the sleepless nights? The damn pounding headaches?"

I knew he sensed my mood change from nice guy who lets everyone shit on you to a raging bull ready to kick ass. My eyes told the story and he'd seen it before. He was a pro at this and for that I respected him. Weed out the asshole bullshitters and REMFs. That was his job. Help the vets like me, the wounded that no one gave a damn about.

"Phil, welcome here. I feel you saw too much in too little time." He shook my hand. I calmed down. "You'll be staffed tomorrow."

"What's that?"

"You'll sit with a group of nurses and staff personnel who'll ask more questions. They'll let you know what you have to work on while you're here."

"Okay. Sorry I lost my temper."

"I understand. You can go now."

I left the doctor's office and headed to my room. My head felt like it was going to explode. I asked a nurse for some aspirin. She checked my chart and handed me two Tylenol. They didn't help. I needed something stronger.

I lay down for a while then got up for dinner. Big Ed walked into my room humming some off-the-wall tune.

"Hey man, you going to chow?"

"Oh, hi Ed. Yeah, I'll go with you," I replied.

I never refused a meal and thought it would help the headache if I ate. I missed lunch and needed something in my stomach. The walk was about a half a mile or so at the other end of the compound. I was lost; it took a few days to figure out where everything was.

When we got to the chow hall there was already a line. Just like the damn Army.

"I hate damn lines. A real cluster fuck, if you know what I

mean," said Big Ed. He reminded me of John Candy.

"I hear ya," piped up Frank as he stepped out of line to be with us.

"They'd better not have gook food. I ain't eating that shit!" said Frank.

Big Ed and I looked at each other. Ed rolled his eyes. We approached the serving line.

"Fuck this, damn rice! Gook food! I can't eat that shit!"

Frank threw his tray back and stormed out of the mess hall. Ed and I stood there not believing our eyes.

"More for me," laughed Ed, all three-hundred-some-odd pounds of him. I'd be heading in the same direction if I didn't watch my diet.

You had to give your name when you got up to be served and show a card. On my card it explained a special diet for high cholesterol, something I hadn't known I had. Almost everyone up on the SRU shared my diagnosis. I was soon to learn I shared a lot more than high cholesterol with my SRU comrades.

Chapter Eight

IT DIDN'T TAKE long to figure everyone out. I learned who the bullshitters were and kept my mouth shut. I also didn't feel comfortable yet telling everyone my life story. The staff already knew what I had been through in 'Nam, and in civilian life as I had struggled with the rating system. It was so important to have someone who finally believed in me.

They told me I was different than many who had walked through the SRU halls. I had no substance abuse or marital problems. But they understood that I needed care because I had served and bled in Vietnam.

Most up on the unit hadn't been physically wounded in 'Nam. When I first got to the hospital I heard someone whisper, "That's the guy with the Purple Heart." Later a couple others came in who had Purple Hearts so I didn't feel like the Lone Ranger anymore.

At the staffing I sat before a panel of doctors and nurses: Dr. Camron, Dr. Meeker, Nurse Linda Beckman and Jim Bedford. Bedford and a few others took notes as I talked. Don and Mike, two male nurses, had their pens going a mile a minute, glancing up occasionally to watch my reactions.

Bedford sat and listened with tears in his eyes. Bedford was a wounded 'Nam vet, a lieutenant with a line company. I already trusted him. It was a grunt kind of connection. He fought the battle and spilled the blood. He knew actually what was going on in my mind. Our eyes often made contact as I spoke.

"I shot at them like it was nothing, man!" I screamed out.

Even though I had bad feelings about shooting people, this had never bothered me before. What I felt needed to come out. "I wasn't raised to kill people. My fingers went numb on the trigger."

My eyes began to tear up as I spoke from the heart. I didn't like shooting people. We had chased them down and had them on the run like they were animals. That bothered me. When someone was looking down a barrel of a damn AK-47, then that was different.

I didn't care who believed me or not anymore. I told them about my experience in Cambodia. They all believed me. I wasn't another bullshitter. I was real. I wasn't the clichéd combat-crazed Vietnam vet.

I left the staff meeting with a migraine headache and mixed up feelings bobbing around in my skull—a skull scarred by shrapnel but scared even deeper with emotion.

✪ ✪ ✪

I WAS INTRODUCED TO my team a couple of days into the program. All the SRU patients were divided into two teams, one lead by Dr. Camron and the other led by Dr. Meeker, a more compassionate man. He visibly hurt as men explained their personal horrors.

I was also assigned a nurse, a one-on-one counselor. Her name was Linda Becker. I had met her at my staffing. She cared deeply about vets and she'd been with the VA for a while. I felt comfortable with her and often shared my thoughts. This is what she wanted you to do. She knew her job.

At first I didn't say much in the group sessions. Trust didn't come easily for me. In 'Nam I only learned to trust a select few. Mostly I had just trusted myself.

That was hard too because at times I did some dumb things. At times my judgment was off. There was no room for that. No mistakes. Mistakes got people killed. Many had died because some asshole didn't know what the hell he was doing.

I remembered a cook who was killed one day because he was put on a detail unloading explosives. The men were throwing boxes of claymore mines to each other off the back of a truck. One blew up and the cook who didn't know what he was handling had died.

I thought a lot about mistakes. My thoughts became clearer to me after a group session. I didn't say any thing for about a week, but my mind was working overtime.

Dr. Meeker saw it. Someone had struck a nerve. We made eye contact. He knew I was thinking about some messed up mission I was on. A man burst out in anger.

"Phil, what do you think about that?" asked Meeker.

I looked up at him. "I can relate. I've messed up."

He nodded and looked at me with steel blue eyes. "How do you feel about that?"

"It pisses me off," I said.

Others sat tight and stared at me. They had been waiting for the Purple Heart guy to open up. I wanted to prove myself but I didn't need to. Suddenly my emotions got the best of me. I needed to speak out.

"Yeah I screwed up. Who the hell didn't?"

Meeker gave me the sign to open up. I knew it was my turn to be in the hot seat.

"I went out to save a guy once," I said. "I saved his ass twice, man. Almost got myself killed. For what? He died anyway!"

Why was my little buddy killed? I couldn't help him anymore. Time ran out. It was in God's hands. I had never accepted that.

Another answer? I was not able to accept the loss of certain friends. This might have been an answer but it still didn't make the pain go away.

"My head hurts," I said. "I don't want to go into it anymore. Not today."

Meeker nodded and the session continued.

The conversation had hit a nerve. Bunny. I still couldn't talk about Bunny without firing off.

I still had seven long hard weeks left in the hospital. Other nerves would be hit. I worried about how I'd handle it. I felt comfortable with the members of the group because they showed me respect. And the men from the other group did too. This was important to me—to be accepted by all. All served in 'Nam; all gave some. I appreciated that and that's all I needed to know. No one had to spill their guts to me. I carried enough luggage around with me and I didn't need someone else's.

I made friends easy as I had in 'Nam. At times that made it hard. Most soldiers learned to keep their circle of friends small. It became too difficult when one got blown away. I remembered some didn't want friends—loners. Mostly the heavy combat ones. I didn't pay attention and became attached to so many guys over in Vietnam.

I hadn't learned my lesson. I felt for some up on the unit. I listened to their life stories and I opened up with them. Was that another problem? I cared for people and that played hell on my mind.

Quickly I realized the buried feelings I had were not that deep. After so many years of trying to come out, they were right at the surface. I needed to talk, but only to those who truly cared.

When our group broke I headed to the restroom. I wanted to just lie down awhile before lunch. Usually we got a little rest between group sessions. They kept you busy though throughout the day—classes on self-esteem, anger control and depression, as well as exercise over in another building with bikes and weights.

As I walked out of the restroom I glanced down the hall to

the alcohol substance abuse ward. I noticed a tall guy with a knee brace and crutches. He had the look of someone that just wanted to be alone. I'd noticed him for the past few days. We'd made eye contact but never said a word to each other.

Frank walked by me. "What's up?"

"Same shit." I took another look down the hall. "That guy looks mad at the world," I said.

"Yeah, that's John, the marine. He'll be over here next week. He's combat. I've talked with him."

"Looks like he's got messed up knees," I said.

"Shrapnel. He got screwed over with the rating system like you."

"Let's take a walk. I've got to get the hell away from here for awhile," I said.

We entered the elevator and saw a couple more guys standing there with suitcases. "SRU?" asked Frank.

"Yes, where is it?"

We gave them directions and headed outside.

"Two more poor grunts," said Frank.

Frank seemed to stay in a perpetual bad mood but our walks calmed him down. Ostensibly the walks were to help me lose a couple extra pounds and Frank strengthen a bum knee, but mostly we just talked a lot about Vietnam.

"How did group go?" asked Frank.

"I started to tell about a friend of mine who was killed."

I figured it would be easier to talk about things with Frank rather than the whole group.

"Want to talk about it? I'm here man. I lived the shit," Frank said in a sympathetic voice.

I tried to explain my relationship with Bunny. I tried to remember the day he came to our platoon, when he died, and the days in the middle. Those were the days I got to know and care about him. It was hard to think of him.

"I can't remember his face," I said, looking down. "He's

the only one."

"Man," Frank said.

"I guess I've blocked him out of my mind. After he died, I still had eight more months in country. I had to go on. No time to mourn."

✪ ✪ ✪

I REMEMBERED THE DAY I met Bunny. We were off for a few days, and everyone was hung over from drinking the night before. A jeep pulled up.

"FNG!" someone yelled.

"Hey man, your replacement on the horn. Now you can walk point," Jerry said, laughing.

"Yeah thanks. You gave me your radio. Want it back?"

"No, that's all right. It fits you," Jerry said as we sauntered over to the new guy.

"Hi. I'm Phil and this is Jerry. Welcome to your new home."

Bunny smiled nervously and shook our hands. He wore that wide-eyed innocent look on his face. We were all green and innocent when we first arrived in Vietnam. I shook my head. Another poor slob drawn into that mud hole.

He didn't talk much and seemed nervous about meeting new friends. I didn't let him stay that way. I'd often go over to talk with him when he looked lonely. After a while he'd come looking for me.

"You're pretty good at that thing," Bunny said one day when he caught me strumming an old guitar that was passed around within the 9th Division. Can't remember how I got it. I guess at the time I was the only one who could play a little.

"Not really," I said, as I practiced the lead to "Pretty Woman." Could never get it quite right. Bunny liked it, though. No matter what I played, he got a kick out of it.

✪ ✪ ✪

"YOU KNOW, I DON'T remember him drinking a damn beer," I said to Frank.

He nodded with a sensitive smile. The tough guy had heart. He knew I needed to talk. That's one thing we understood about each other. When one guy needed to open up the other would listen.

"He had a hell of a time in the bush, always getting his ass stuck in the mud."

✪ ✪ ✪

THEY DROPPED US into an area that had just been bombed. Everything was destroyed. The trees were all blown apart. We walked through mud and water all day, hot as a bitch. Single file we made our way over twisted and bent trees.

"Where's Bunny?" I asked.

No one answered.

Bunny kept falling back farther and farther. No one paid attention. Minutes earlier we had heard a mini gun from a chopper letting off bursts. Then more bursts and they were closer to our rear. Those damn mini guns could cover a large area.

"Man, where is he?" I asked again.

"We gotta get the fuck out of here!" someone yelled. The gun was hitting too damn close.

"We can't go back," another said. The squad started to move faster, almost at a run.

"We gotta get Bunny," I screamed.

"We can't!" yelled another.

I was so mad because no one was watching out for Bunny. It was difficult enough being the new guy. Carrying the pack and heavy ammo in the heat was doubly exhausting for a FNG.

Humping your ass through fucking mud sucked at your very soul. It extracted your free will. After a while you had the feeling you were part of the 'Nam. You were the mud, the shit. You smelled like it, you slept in it, and when the shit hit the fan, you ate it. The lousy smelly crap went down your throat, gook piss and all.

Somebody had to watch out for Bunny.

I headed off away from the squad, into where the mini gun was firing. I must have been nuts. I had the radio and started to scream over it to get someone to stop the mini guns. I can't remember, exactly. I just remember screaming.

I retraced my steps and found Bunny hanging over a downed tree. His shirt had caught on a branch. He was out of breath and his face was red as hell. He had a defeated look in his eyes.

"You all right, Bunny?" I asked as the guns sprayed the area.

He didn't even have enough strength left in him to talk.

It was like back in basic training—when that drill sergeant came around you drew the strength from some damn place. If you didn't, you'd get a boot up your ass.

But this wasn't basic. This was hell.

I took some of his gear and unhooked him. "Come on, man! We gotta get the hell outta here!"

He moved faster than I ever saw him move. All he needed was a guy who cared about him.

Somehow we made it back to the squad, up to our knees in jungle muck, but still in once piece.

✪ ✪ ✪

FRANK SHOOK HIS head. "That's some fucking story."

"Can we talk later?" I asked. "This stuff is getting to me."

"No sweat. Let's get back. We have to go to a class. They

have a movie for us to watch. I think about The Wall."

"Oh great, that should mess my mind up for the remainder of the day." We walked back.

Watching movies about Vietnam upset me. I could picture myself right back in 'Nam, just like it was yesterday. Most felt that way. Some got emotional and cried. Some would walk out of the room when something upset them.

We talked of those who never made it back. Many couldn't remember their buddies—faces, names, nothing.

That wasn't my case. I remembered them all, so when I lost someone, he had been my friend. The guys who had been in country longest warned us not to get too close. I never listened. I got close, over and over.

We'd constantly hear about Americans back home protesting. The war was wrong and many said we were wrong for being there. After a while it sucked at me, just like the mud. If the people back home weren't on our side, who was?

I always had God, although some said they lost faith in him. At times some really thought there was no God. I thanked God everyday and never lost the feeling there was a god.

But I would question him. And I would get angry with him. I didn't want to, and I felt guilty. Maybe that was another unanswered screwed up question? Could God forgive me for being angry with him? Could I ever forgive God for the atrocities of war?

Nights up on the ward, I'd find myself sitting up in a small library at the end of the hall. Sometimes I'd sit in the bathroom where guys would stay up all night. They'd smoke, talk about 'Nam, and how to deal with the VA.

There were some good shithouse lawyers up there. Many had been through the program two or three times. They'd get service connected for PTSD, wait a year, go back in and pick up more on their percentage rating.

It didn't seem fair that simply knowing how to work the

system could get one guy a better rating than another who was shot up.

Spending twelve months on the line without a scratch could fuck you up pretty quickly too. You lived with guilt and the fear of waiting your turn to get wounded or killed.

Would it be a booby trap, a sniper, or a kid handing you a grenade with the damn pin pulled?

After twelve months of sick anticipation, even getting on the plane could fuck with you. You just knew the Freedom Bird was gonna blow. It never ended. They scared the living hell out of you in basic, you shit your pants in a firefight, and then you carried the nervous feeling around in your stomach for the rest of your life.

✪ ✪ ✪

"PHIL, YOU GOT A call," shouted an orderly.

I walked to the large room where we would meet every morning for doctor's rounds. Dr. Camron would ask each person if anything was bothering him. Everyone bitched about something. If he felt your complaint wasn't justified, you caught it. He'd make you feel as low as whale shit.

One guy complained about a headache every time. He jumped him so bad that the guy wanted to quit the program. He made him stay—I think just to torment him more.

"Hello," I said, taking the phone.

"Yeah man, it's me Dan." Dan had been nervous ever since I entered the hospital. "You want me to break you out?" he asked.

"No, it's not like that. I can leave if I want. After a few weeks I can even go home on weekends."

"No shit. Can I come up to visit you?"

"Yeah man, at eight o'clock."

"Okay, I'll come on up. Need anything?"

"No."

I told him how to get back to where I was, and then we hung up.

I headed out of the building around eight knowing Dan would be driving up. I spotted him walking toward the building as I stepped out of the elevator.

"Hey, you dumb shit," he said as he passed others sitting around smoking. His hat read "Vietnam Vet" and his t-shirt had a map of 'Nam and a 9th Division patch on it. He had a halting gait and it was pretty easy to see that he was as fucked up as anyone already up on the ward.

"Let's walk," I said.

"How ya doin'? They treating you okay?"

"Oh yeah, it ain't bad. I'm screwed up worse than I thought. 'Nam did a number on me."

"I know I'm messed up, but I think you're worse," said Dan.

My stomach curled. Dan suffered from combat trauma and I had always thought he should be there with me. When I had told him I was going in he became tense and anxious. We both had a feeling of uncertainty over me going into the program.

We walked to the dock out back and talked about what it was like in the hospital, and of course about 'Nam. We've never had a conversation that didn't include Vietnam, and it always left both of us jumpy.

I tried to avoid talking about it but it never did any good. I listened to him many times as he recalled the horrifying situations he had gotten himself into. If he needed me to listen, then I was there for him. Now he was there for me. We both knew what we had faced in 'Nam and it formed a bond that no one could break.

"Remember back in advanced infantry training when you got pissed at that lieutenant and swung at him?" asked Dan.

✪ ✪ ✪

I COULD NEVER FORGET that day. It was a miserable wet day on the rifle range. It was close to the end of AIT and we all knew we'd be sent to Vietnam. On Christmas leave I went home and Kathy and I were married. It was a very hard time for us and our families.

That day I lay on the ground shooting my M-16. I had to learn how to shoot it because my life someday might depend on it. I was not in the mood to accommodate some asshole second lieutenant who hadn't been to 'Nam yet either. His ass was as green as mine.

I took aim, firing magazine after magazine, learning how to quickly insert one after another. Suddenly I felt a boot to my ribs.

"What's in your mouth?" asked a tall, heavy-set, fresh-out-of-some-ninety-day-wonder-school-that-qualified-him-to-know-everything-about-war-and-the-'Nam lieutenant.

"Gum, sir!" I shouted back, not appreciating the kick.

"You're not authorized to chew gum. Take it out and stick it on your nose, then go back to shooting."

"Fuck me," I mumbled. What an asshole. Didn't he have anything better to do?

But I did what he said. Moments later the gum fell off my nose and into the sawdust I was laying on.

"Oh man," I said as I panicked searching for the gum.

He spotted me and forced his hand against the back of my neck.

I swung around, and when I did, he caught a forearm across the throat. I jumped up and cussed him out.

"If you ever touch me again, I'll kill you!" I screamed at the top of my lungs.

He turned white, figuring he might have bit off a little too much this time. And he had. I was trained now, and in my current state of mind, I didn't care what happened. If I went to jail, who cared? Better than going to 'Nam.

Ready for something to happen to me, I noticed a captain walking over to us.

"Sir," said the young officer.

He started to open his mouth and the captain, a 'Nam vet, jumped deep into this guy's shit.

"Say you're sorry to this private," the captain said. "I saw the whole thing."

The second lieutenant's face flushed and his lips tightened.

"Sorry," he said.

It was over. For now. I knew he had ways to get back at me, but I knew he wouldn't try because he knew deep inside if he ever laid a hand on me, that was it, officer or not.

The morale was low and others were starting to feel the same. Hell, we weren't even in 'Nam yet. Fort Polk had been nothing but hell from the moment we arrived to the day we left. Now I realized why. It was their job. They wanted us to hate the damn place. They knew what was ahead of us in 'Nam would be far worse.

Sandy was now assigned to a desk job, because of his feet. Dan, Dave, Harvey and myself—all from Clearwater—waited for the word. Sandy would see the orders come down. One night we got the not-surprising news. We all knew we would, but still there was this little ray of hope that we wouldn't.

"You're all going, man," Sandy said stiffly. "I'm sorry."

"When?" I asked.

"February."

It almost felt good knowing we'd be getting out of Polk. That was a sick way of looking at it, but it was true. We had Christmas leave, and then we would only get ten days leave before shipping out to Vietnam. That was hard, and the ten days felt like one.

As we prepared for graduation from AIT, we proudly put

on our dress greens. We hated it yet we had some pride for what we had accomplished. We were infantry, ready to serve our country.

"Where the hell do you guys think you're going?" barked the sergeant walking into the barracks. His damn Smokey-the-Bear hat almost covered his eyes.

"To the parade," I said.

"Look, we want the parade to look good. You guys are too short."

We all stood five eight or less. My height never bothered me. Hell, I almost maxed the physical training test. What the hell bullshit were they trying to hand us now? They wanted to break us down to make us feel worthless, to demoralize us.

They did a good job of it. As the platoon walked in a parade we were folding blankets in the supply room. The funny thing is that I think we were the only ones heading to Vietnam. They screwed with us from start to finish.

✪ ✪ ✪

"GOTTA GO, BUDDY," Dan finally said, shaking my hand. We must have shook hands a thousand times. Every time we parted we wondered if we would ever see each other again. This time was no different. It has never changed. We changed over there, but never changed back.

I wanted the feelings I had before I went to war. Was that possible? After over twenty years I was afraid I knew the answer. Forget it asshole, you're changed forever and the only thing that can change you back is having your mind fucked back into reverse somehow. Some sort of shock? That's what they used to do—electric shock. No way would they strap my butt into a chair with some asshole I didn't know fiddling with the switch.

I walked back to the ward as Dan drove off. He was

smiling and so was I. *We're so messed up*, I thought.

"Ain't this a bitch?" I said to myself as I waved. It was dark and the sidewalk was long. I looked to the stars and talked to them, like I did years ago. I wasn't lying in a rice paddy this time. That was one good thing.

Half way through SRU, I knew some answers. I had the feeling I would break down soon. I had to get out my anger. I listened to others.

In SRU, I grew close to others who shared my feelings. We were a unit. I was part of a team again. Maybe I liked that because after I was wounded I had been separated from my buddies.

We were told to write down our thoughts and feelings in a little notebook they gave us. I found myself comparing the guys in SRU to guys I served with in 'Nam.

"Dammit," I cried out to the stars. "Someone will hear me before this is over!"

Chapter Nine

AS MY TWO-MONTH stay in SRU drew to a close, I found myself anxious to get on with my life.

I was worried though; I had no desire to resurrect my construction company. The pain was worse and still I had no answers for it. I believed the doctors wanted me to admit that the pain I was suffering was from PTSD. An upper GI test showed nothing, but the pain was real. There were times the staff would witness it. The sleepless nights and the constant migraine headaches were easy to see. My mood would change when the pain got worse. I wanted to think at least the staff believed me, even though the medical doctors didn't seem concerned.

I became quiet toward the end, feeling sad about leaving friends again. This time I had the chance to say goodbye—not like in Vietnam.

The way I was comparing the guys to ones I left behind was another thing that was messing up my head. John and I became close. His look reminded me of Sergeant Williams, my protector in the war. The one who broke me in. I was lucky. He was the best. He didn't like everybody. John was like that. He also spoke his mind, like Williams. He had a "You don't like what I say? Then fuck you!" type of attitude. Tough as hell, but I could see his compassionate side. They both had it and they both shared it with me. This is what made them real and genuine. Good soldiers were like that. They were the kind you wanted next to you when the shit hit. I had that with Williams.

Williams had been a big part of my Vietnam tour. I

thought about him more and more. I lay down at night and he was on my mind. I remembered when I first met him, and how he looked out for me. I smiled when I thought of him. But it would break my heart when I thought of how he died.

I didn't have the chance to say thanks, much less goodbye. I had to say it as I touched his name on The Wall.

✪ ✪ ✪

WHEN I FIRST ARRIVED in Vietnam I was separated from my hometown friends. It devastated me. I remember walking guard duty the night before I was going to be sent to my combat unit. Alone and scared, I paced back and forth in front of the administration building at the headquarters company.

I saw caskets set up, ready for delivery back to the States. I couldn't avoid looking; it was reality, and I was there. I had nobody to confide in. No more jokes. It was me and the stars.

I looked up. The tears came and I prayed to God to protect me. I needed to get home to my young wife. I couldn't make her a widow. The thought of it put so much pain in my heart. Maybe I shouldn't have gotten married. Was it fair to Kathy?

I had her on my mind as I spoke to God. I remembered my last day at home. My parents drove us across the Tampa Causeway to the airport that early morning. Kathy and I sat in the back seat. We hardly said a word. We listened to the songs on the radio and no one talked.

"Well, we made it, honey," I said looking at just one star. "I'm in 'Nam now but I'll be home before you know it. Don't worry."

It was hard to believe we were married only two months when I first arrived to my combat unit. We were married on December 22, 1969. We wanted to do it on Valentines Day, but that was the day I arrived in Vietnam. I kept talking to myself and to the star, taking deep breaths.

I hadn't even looked back that gloomy early morning. I kissed everyone goodbye. I walked to the plane and never looked back. Many times during my tour, I often regretted I didn't take another peek. What good would it have done? None, probably. And maybe it would have made it harder.

In my mind, I prepared to meet my new unit. I had no choice but to go on. I couldn't walk home or say, "I quit." Hell, how many other guys were lucky enough to do this? They'd have to wonder the rest of their lives, "What was it like?" They'd never know.

The lucky shits.

Not their faults. We all had our own destiny. What would be my outcome?

The jeep slowed, pulling up to bring me to my combat unit.

"Come on, soldier," said a grim-looking dark-tanned guy in a worn-out jungle hat. Half his teeth were missing.

I could tell he had a lot of months in country. The eyes always gave you away. And your boots. The more worn out, the more months you had been there, or the fewer months you had left to do. I figured when the boots wore out it was time to go.

My eyes gave me away too. I was ready to do something in my pants and hadn't even shot a round yet.

The ride was long and bumpy to Tan Tru, south of Saigon. We pulled up to a company area where a sign read, "Alpha Company, 2nd Battalion, 60th Infantry, 9th Division, Old Reliables."

Gee, I thought, *Hope I don't let anyone down, might be some big shoes to follow.*

This was a kick ass division. They used boats, ACVs (air-cushioned vehicles) and of course helicopters for the famous eagle flights. They'd drop us anywhere they thought the Vietcong were. And it didn't matter if you landed in a mud hole up to your neck.

Within a month I had enough combat insertions to qualify for the Air Medal. After the first month, I already had my Combat Infantryman Badge. The CIB was an honor respected in the Army. You wore that and you thought you were really something.

Didn't mean shit twenty years later.

To my surprise, live ammo lay all around the barracks. The barracks had been constructed of ammo boxes and sand bags. It was divided off into little rooms or hootches. Two grunts to a hootch.

Confederate flags hung all over. Loud country music blasted out as soldiers chugged beer like there was no tomorrow. The men had just come in from a mission and it was time to kick back. Days earlier several had been killed by a booby-trap so a somber mood shown on the faces of almost all.

"Here's a beer, man," said a tall sandy-haired guy.

"Thanks. I'm from Florida," I said.

"Yeah? Me too. What part?"

"Clearwater."

"I'm from Orlando. Nice having you, man. I'm Vic, carry the sixty." The sixty was a machine gun.

"Thanks," I said, still nervous about my new surroundings. I worried about what the hell I'd be carrying.

When I saw all the Confederate flags, I thought I'd better say I was from Florida instead of New York.

"All right, another rebel boy!" yelled someone.

Music and smoke filled the air as I glanced around. "Midnight Cowboy" played on a radio. I noticed the words to songs had more meaning. The songs had you longing for home. They made you need to make it back.

I was made welcome, but was lonely. After all, I was the FNG. I knew I had to prove myself. They didn't owe me a thing. They'd been living in the 'Nam longer than my green butt. I thought I'd better keep my mouth shut and listen to the ones who knew what they were doing. That's what I'd always heard—listen to the ones who have been through it. It could help you stay alive.

Soon I met Bill, my hootch-mate. "Man, you have a New York accent, don't sound like Florida. I'm from Ohio, been here a couple of weeks," he said.

"Born in New York but moved to Florida when I was ten. Guess I never lost the accent."

We both laughed and hit it off right away.

"You have the lower bunk," he said.

I gave it a funny look. The lower bunk only had a spring and the top bunk was only a couple feet above it. "Where's the mattress?"

Bill laughed. "You'll hardly use it. We're always out in the bush. It's not bad right now. Kind of dry in the paddies. You take a bunch of straw and lie on it. When it starts raining, then that's gonna be some shit."

"How the hell you get used to this place?"

"Don't worry, man. I'll show you around."

We stuck together like glue. I was lucky. Bill was a good guy, and we looked out for each other. On patrol I initially walked drag, the end of the line. Bill carried the "Thumper," the M-79 grenade launcher. It fired a forty-millimeter high explosive round and was a very effective weapon. Bill felt comfortable with it and knew how to use it. No one could carry the M-60 machine gun like Willie and Vic. We all took turns with different weapons. Eventually you wound up with the one that fit you the best.

Then there was the point man, a breed of his own— adventurous, alert, eyes always wide open, scanning every inch in front of him. Their M-16s were always pointed straight— trigger-ready. Point men were mostly volunteers. I did it a few times and I didn't like it, flat out.

Jerry broke me in on the radio and that's where I wound up. I didn't like that either, but that's what I did best. I took my job seriously. At times someone's life depended on how the RTO reacted. They trusted me, and I owed it to every one to be there if I was needed.

A true test was when you had to perform. Could I?

"Wait till you meet Williams. He'll be back from R & R today," said Bill. "He's our platoon sergeant and he knows his stuff. Second tour."

"Who'd want to come here twice?" I said.

"Can't figure that one out myself."

"Who was he with on his first tour?"

"The 4th Division. They caught the hell. He don't talk much. A big guy—you don't want to piss his ass off. Everybody likes him but he doesn't get too close to anyone."

He hasn't met me yet, I thought. I couldn't wait to meet this guy who was sounding like a soldier's soldier, a legend among men—the guy you wanted next to you when you were in trouble.

Williams' first words to me were "Keep your head out of your ass and keep your shit together."

He was a huge guy, a little overweight, but solid as a brick wall. He acted like he was always pissed off. His round, rosy-cheeked baby-face still had some baby fat. His jet-black hair always looked groomed but sweaty. At twenty-one, he was already an E6. He must have been in some deep shit to make E6 that early.

Little by little we became closer. He started treating me like a kid brother.

One starry night, just as it became dark, we lay along a dike in a wet rice paddy.

"Come on," Williams said to me, pointing to a few huts off in the distance. The squad stayed while we made it to the grass huts. Williams knocked on the door of a hut.

"What the fuck you doin'?" I asked.

He smiled. "I want to get something to eat."

"Are you kidding me?"

The door opened and he started talking in Vietnamese, as if he had graduated from Saigon High School. They welcomed us in as if we were long lost relatives. I didn't know what they were saying, but they were laughing and looking at me.

The whole family sat around a table on a dirt floor. These were peasant farmers and had very little but were ready to offer us a meal. Their eyes were sad but had a glow to them.

The old *mama san* smiled at me and I could see only red in her mouth. They chewed this betel nut stuff to kill the pain in their teeth. I figured their looks far exceeded their true ages.

"We have to eat now or they'll get offended," said a grinning Williams.

"What?" A bowl of rice and fish heads, eyes and all, sat before me.

Williams was eating like all-get-out and sucking down some homemade rice wine.

I took a drink and it almost sent me all the way to Hanoi.

They all laughed at me. I joined in—why not? It was good entertainment. And it was my first glimpse of the Vietnamese culture. They seemed to be a happy people. It was sad to see how they had to cope with the war.

Williams had been hardcore and a true warrior and he loved what he was doing. He was also among the few that cared for the people. That night while we ate, he acted like he was one of them. I saw something in him others didn't. He let his guard down with me. He had a heart and he needed to escape the war at times, like we all did. We became close. Williams continued to look out for me. One day his compassion put him in danger.

As we were humping through a swamp, we heard the crack of M-16s and AK-47s up ahead. The squad in front of us had made contact.

"Come on!" ordered Williams. He wanted to get to where the action was. Not me, but I did what he said.

We had to cross a stream. As I swam, the weight from the radio pulled me down. I was almost to the bank when I went under, gasping for air in the muddy waters of the 'Nam. I thought I was going to drown. I heard the crackling gunfire while I was under the water. I was certain I was going to die.

Suddenly a big hand pulled me to the bank. Williams. I spat up murky water as I thanked him.

He uttered not a word, but his resolve showed through. He wanted to make it to the next squad. He wanted to do his job. He was the true warrior—the kind you idolized in books and movies.

We approached the action and could see soldiers pointing their weapons into holes filled with Viet Cong. Some were dead.

More cracks ripped through the humid air. Williams pushed me to the ground. The VC were still popping out of the holes.

The RTO Jon Sapp took a bullet and jerked to the ground.

My first dead GI.

Enraged, Williams fired magazine after magazine into the hole as he walked right up to it. He never once let up. His M-16 stayed pointed.

I couldn't believe it. He wasn't thinking of his own safety. He was pissed about Sapp.

We took some prisoners and they weren't treated well. Some just wanted to kill them.

"Waste the bastards!" someone shouted.

Oh man, I thought. My fish eyes and rice turned over in my stomach. I was going to witness a murder.

Evener heads prevailed, though, and the prisoners were spared.

"Man, are you nuts," I said to Williams, shaking my head.

Again, Williams was silent. Guys who did second tours did it because of their first tour. Unfinished business.

I realize now he had all the symptoms of post-traumatic stress disorder. No one knew about it then.

When we became involved in Cambodia and I was the battalion RTO, Williams was in charge of another platoon. We had Sergeant Washington. His attitude was similar to Williams' and he also had returned for a second tour.

Two weeks after I was wounded I heard Williams had been killed. He died assaulting holes like he had that day with me. This time a machine gun cut my buddy up. I wasn't there, but I could see it in my mind. I was numb when I heard about it. Guilt wracked my body. If I had been there, maybe I could have talked him out of doing it. I doubt it, though. He did what he wanted.

Williams died on June 14, 1970—Flag Day. I was discharged from the Army exactly one year later. If any day could be thought of as an appropriate day to die, Flag Day would be it for a man who gave so much for his country.

Every year when that flag goes up, I salute it for Dale Williams, a true hero. Every June 14th I remember the day I got out, and most importantly, I remember my hard-as-nails, baby-faced platoon sergeant with a good heart. I knew a real hero of the Vietnam War. I wondered if the country he died for realized it.

✪ ✪ ✪

THINKING OF WILLIAMS was sure hard on me, and I still had the others to grieve for. Each held a special place in my heart.

Bunny was on my mind as I thought about Williams, and those in SRU knew his death affected me. They encouraged me to talk it out, but I wasn't sure I would deal that hand out to these guys. I thought maybe I should hold something back, that I should keep them all guessing. They already heard how I saved Bunny once. They knew he died next to me along with Washington. I mentioned it to Joe. Maybe that was enough.

Usually your last few days on the unit you'd have to talk about things in group that had been bothering you.

"Tell us about Bunny," one guy said.

I just looked at him. "Fuck you," I spat.

I didn't know why I said that. Too personal? Too touchy? I knew I didn't like anyone telling me what to say. If I wanted to say something, it was my business. I guess that was another piece of the puzzle; I couldn't take orders anymore.

As I calmed down I realized he had asked me about Bunny because I'd be leaving soon. If I needed to get something out, I had one last chance.

I decided to talk.

"Maybe he pissed me off," I said. "The whole fuckin' thing pissed me off!"

✪ ✪ ✪

I TOLD OF THE first day we got into Cambodia. We were so tired that night. It was a very dark night—hell you couldn't see your hand in front of your face. We dug in for the night and sent out our listening posts—Bunny, Orgeron, and Smitty. They were all new, but were good guys. Orgeron seemed to have his act together better than most. He and Smitty came over together. You couldn't separate them. They were like bookends.

As the night went on, it became very still and quiet. I was getting calls in every half hour then it stopped. I tried to make contact over the radio with the LP but got no response.

I woke Washington.

"Hey man, the guys on LP stopped calling in."

"How long ago?"

"I don't know, a while."

We tried again. Nothing.

"Take someone and go find them."

"What?" Was he kidding me? Unfortunately, no. He was serious. Jerry and Bill woke up and crawled over to my hole.

"What's up?" Jerry asked.

I told him.

"Fuck that shit."

"No way," said Bill. "What the hell did I tell you when you first got here? Don't volunteer man."

"I didn't. He ordered me."

I didn't know what to do. They could be out there in the night with their throats cut. It had happened before. We were in deep NVA country and they were better trained than we were. They moved at night as we slept.

I had to go out and find them. I took Dutchess, another FNG. Jerry stayed on the radio and Bill stayed awake with him. I was told to go. I didn't want either one of them going with me unless they wanted to. I would have felt better if one would have, but Dutchess didn't complain.

"I can't believe you're doing this," Bill said. "Watch yourself."

I was worried about Bunny. I threw on a couple bandoleers of M-16 ammo and my M-16 and headed out with Dutchess. Without the radio hanging on my back, I felt light, almost naked.

We had no idea how far out they went out. If it were me I'd only go out fifty yards and lie down. At times I stopped even closer in. These guys were all new and probably went out a lot farther.

In the moonlight we found a wisp of a trail. We followed the eerie trail until it ended in a grassy clearing with downed trees. We kept walking, Dutchess in back of me ready to shit his pants. I think I already had but didn't want to alarm him. He thought I was a bad-ass because I was friends with Williams.

"Where the fuck are they?" I muttered. My heart raced. I just knew they were dead and some gook bastard was sitting there waiting for some stupid GI son-of-a-bitch to come out looking for them.

Oh man, why this shit? We were walking at a crawl; I could see a tree down and what looked like three steel pots lined neatly in a row.

"Look, maybe that's them," I whispered.

If they were alive we had to be careful not to startle them. If they were dead, we had to watch out for booby traps.

"Orgeron," I called out softly. His name wasn't common so he would think it was one of us. I hoped.

"Orgeron, Orgeron," I repeated as we approached.

Still nothing.

Now I could make out three bodies. My heart pounded as we approached.

I bent down and touched one.

The body jumped.

I had scared the living day lights out of Bunny. The other two woke up.

"What the fuck are you assholes doin'?" I asked. They knew they were in trouble.

"Sorry, man," they said in unison.

"Yeah you're sorry all right. You want your damn throats cut?" I whispered harshly. "And what about us? We were ordered out here to check on your lame asses. We could have gotten our tails shot off." I was fuming. "Stay awake. We're going back."

I was pissed, but relieved knowing they were alive. I was not thinking clearly and I never should have stormed out like that. Taking a new guy was even worse. I didn't know how he'd react if something happened, much less how I would react. You didn't know until something actually happened. And a person might not react the same way every time. Who the hell knew anything?

We came across a fork in the trail that I didn't remember passing earlier.

"Which way?" Dutchess asked.

"I think here," I said.

"No this one," he said, thumbing towards the right fork.

"Maybe you're right. I'm fucked up after this shit," I said.

We took his way. It seemed like we were walking much too long.

"We took the wrong damn way, Dutchess!" I hissed.

"Sorry, man."

"It ain't your fault. This damn bullshit is really getting to me." We continued on in the same direction. We figured the trail would meet up with the other one.

My gut twisted. Something didn't feel right.

"Stop," I said. We hit the ground looking at each other. "Look, we're walking up on the other side of our own perimeter. They might not know we're out here, unless Jerry and Bill told them. We might walk into one of our own LP's or a fuckin' claymore. We've got to sneak in," I said.

"Are you shitting me?" Dutchess whispered, almost crying.

"Take it easy. We'll make it."

"We should have gone the way you said."

"It's okay. I wasn't sure myself."

My heart was deep into my belly. I didn't want to let on how bad our situation was. I didn't want to die, and I'd be damned if I wanted to die by the guns of our own.

My eyes had adjusted to the darkness and I could tell we were definitely up on the wrong side. I could actually see heads sticking up in foxholes.

"Now I know what a gook feels like, Dutchess," I whispered.

"This is weird," he said. "Does this shit happen all the time?"

"What shit?"

"Having to wake guys up on LP."

"Hell no. This is the first I've ever heard of it. I ain't gonna do it again, I'll tell you that."

"What are we gonna do now?"

"We'll walk in low and slow. When we get close enough we'll try and get someone's attention without getting our sorry asses blown away. Don't worry."

I was telling Dutchess not to worry and I was ready to shit my pants. The damn meatballs and beans I had for my dinner were giving me gas. One loud fart and it might have been, "See ya, stupid GI."

We walked almost straight in. It was easier than I thought. Every stupid ass who was supposed to be on guard was asleep.

I spent the next half hour or so waking guys up. I went over to my position where Jerry and Bill were waiting for me.

I walked up to their backs. "Hey fuck-heads!"

"What the hell, what happened?" asked Bill.

"You won't believe it. What a time."

✪ ✪ ✪

"THE CAPTAIN THANKED me that night," I blasted out. "For what? Being a dumb ass? I saved Bunny's life twice." My voice shook as I fought back tears. "And he goddamned died any-fucking-way."

Chapter Ten

THAT NIGHT AFTER my emotional day in group session, Jerry confronted me. He seldom spoke in group. An ex-marine, he worked on a police force somewhere out west. He seemed older than most of us. He had a full head of gray hair combed back from his forehead. His eyes were perpetually sad, and he stayed alone, talking to no one. But not that night. That night, he talked to me.

"You know Phil, you made me think of something when you were talking about your friend Bunny. It's something that has been eating at me for a long time," he said. "Can we talk outside? I've got to tell someone."

"Sure," I said.

We walked out to the dock. It was already dark. People seemed to open up more in the dark of night. Men were restless, and dealing with 'Nam all day screwed up your head.

"You talked about your dead friend," Jerry began.

Why me? I thought. I was dealing with my own feelings and didn't know if I could handle someone else's.

Jerry talked more than I ever heard him talk before. I guess he figured I could relate to his situation.

"I was delivering a truck," Jerry said. "I was driving and there was a guy sitting in the back. We hit an ambush. I floored it while the guy in back was shooting.

"Then there was no shooting and I couldn't turn around to see what was going on. 'Shoot, dammit!' I screamed at the guy in the back. With the gas pedal pressed to the floor, I cussed the guy out.

"When I thought it was safe, I stopped the truck. I looked to the back of the truck and the guy was gone."

Jerry's voice cracked. "He must have fallen out. The gooks took him."

"What did you do?" I asked.

"I reported to the captain.

"'Get your ass back down the road and find him,' he said. 'We don't leave any marines behind!'"

Jerry hung his head and cried.

I didn't know what to do. "Does the staff know this story?" I asked.

"No, just you."

I was surprised that he had opened up to me. "What happened then?"

"I went back. I drove a couple miles, scared out of my fucking mind. I couldn't believe this asshole had told me to go back."

"Did you find him?"

"Fuck no! I never knew what happened to him. I didn't know if he was killed or what. I'll never know. I was cussing this poor guy out and the damn gooks probably had him. I'm an ass, man."

"You couldn't help it," I said resting a hand on his shoulder. "It wasn't your fault."

I wanted to ease his pain, but knew too many years had passed. What could I say that would have made any sense? Nothing. Sometimes you were left dealing with a traumatic memory and that was the way it was. Some men might never accept their traumas and would take them to their graves.

"Look, I'm leaving in two days," I said. "You should tell someone. You've been here now over a month without a word. I know that if you want help then you've got to tell someone what's going on with you. If you don't, they'll think your problems are not war-related. Unless you talk to somebody, you'll get no help, no compensation, no nothing."

I tried to help him understand that he had to release some of his guilt and anger.

He shook his head and agreed with me.

"Go tell the nurse on duty. She's nice, I've talked with her before," I said.

"I can't. Not right now."

"Do you want me to?"

"If you want," he said in a low voice.

I knew he was in no shape to talk to anyone. I also didn't want his story on my mind. If I could help him, I would.

Inside I found the nurse. "Can we talk?" I asked.

"Sure," she replied eagerly.

I walked into her room and closed the door. Of course everyone was wondering what I was doing.

"Look, I just talked with Jerry."

"He's a hard nut to crack," she said.

"I know one thing that's been bothering him." I told her what Jerry told me. The nurse took notes the entire time.

"Thanks," she said. "I know you have enough of your own to deal with. You're a caring person and these guys look up to you."

I sat there amazed in what she told me.

"You have to learn how to worry about yourself," she said. "I know at times it's not easy, but you're ready to go home and you're going to have a lot to think about. Don't take other people's baggage home with you."

She was right. In 'Nam I did the same. I always tried to look out for others and now I was doing it again. Some things never changed.

It wasn't bad that I cared about others, but the fact was, I never thought about my own wellbeing.

It was time I did. Not only for me, but also for my wife and daughter.

I left and went to bed. I could feel another headache coming on. My most recent VA rating decision didn't help. I had submitted a claim for increases for my wounds and for a service connection for PTSD. Earlier that week I was told I had been denied in all areas. Being on the stress unit and my meetings with Joe didn't mean anything to them. I felt they truly didn't care. The people who were now treating me did, but it was out of their hands. I knew I had to find a way to make the rating board listen.

✪ ✪ ✪

THE DAY CAME FOR me to leave. Usually you would have to stand up and say your goodbyes in front of the staff and everyone. I was emotional about leaving, and wasn't looking forward to this.

I got out of it because every Monday, Wednesday, and Friday morning I had a standing appointment with the audio department for the ringing in my ears. My ears had been ringing ever since the mortar attack, and the stress made it worse.

The audio department had some caring doctors who wanted to help, but one doctor was at his wit's end with me. I worked with biofeedback equipment and would sit in a booth listening to relaxation tapes. Nothing worked, but I tried.

"I can't do a thing with you," the doctor said. "You're one of the worst cases I've ever had."

I never realized I was that bad. Now the recent VA rating decision felt even more like a slap in the face. How could I calm down? I wanted to stay angry until I got what I deserved.

Saying my goodbyes that last day in the hospital was difficult. Almost in tears, I shook everybody's hand. We all said we'd keep in touch, and with some I have.

I struggled relating each guy to the ones I knew in 'Nam.

But who was *I* like? I had to fit into the picture too.

As I shook hands with Jim Bedford, the social worker who also was a wounded veteran, I figured it out. I was like *him*. That's why it took me so long. I wasn't like one of the patients; I was like a staff member. I shared Jim's care and concern for the wellbeing of those around him, and I was sure that, like me, his journey had begun in 'Nam.

The most important thing I learned in SRU was that I was a person who put myself aside to care for others. This didn't make me a bad person. It made me a person who had put his own feelings and thoughts of Vietnam on hold—on hold until I couldn't handle it any longer.

I hid behind my wounds to justify my inability to work anymore. Now I understood that it wasn't all physical pain that was bothering me and that was hard to admit.

But now I learned that I wasn't alone and I had the courage to come forward and face the fact that although my wounds pained me, I was also hurting for what I had experienced in Vietnam. The nightmares and sleepless nights had a reason, and PTSD was one of the causes.

I said goodbye to nurse Linda Becker, my one-on-one counselor.

"Can I have a hug?" she asked.

"Sure," I said.

"You know, I never had anyone up here like you. Everyone looked up to you."

I choked back my tears.

I walked into Dr. Camron's office next. He jumped to his feet. "Phil, it's been a pleasure. Good luck to you."

A firm handshake was all it took for me to realize he respected me, and my ordeal in Vietnam. He wrote a report about me that detailed the horrible events I witnessed in combat. It also said that although my wounds bothered me, I used them as a way to save face for not working. He said I needed hospital care for both pain and PTSD. He mentioned how I wept openly while explaining about those I left behind. He wrote about my visit to The Wall. At the end his diagnosis—PTSD, chronic.

The road was winding now with no turning back. I was as confused as when I faced that fork in the trail that crazy night in Cambodia. Which direction should I choose?

But unlike that night in Cambodia, I knew the answer: the path that would lead to the proper rating from the VA, for me and my family. It wasn't just for me. It was important to think of them. We were as one and they were my responsibility. Taking care of myself would be taking care of them. I resolved to stand and fight at all costs.

I drove home in tears, not from regret or sadness, but from relief. So many emotions had been uncovered, and yet I now felt I had a purpose in life—to be recognized for my wounds, and for the trauma I had endured because of Vietnam.

I knew my new road ahead of me was going to be a tough one. Could I endure an ongoing struggle? I wasn't sure. But I knew that if I had to die trying then that's the way it had to be. I knew I was right to fight for full compensation. Others had thought the same, and it made it a little easier.

The plan for me was weekly meetings with Joe at the Vet Center, plus one night a week in group sessions. And something new—a stop at the mental health clinic for meds.

This upset me at first, but I knew it had to be done. I needed to calm down before other problems occurred. Someone could be hurt, or I could hurt myself.

What I had learned from SRU and what others had been through scared me. I realized I couldn't trust myself anymore if my temper got the best of me. I came close to giving up, but the hate and anger and deep love for my family kept me going. To keep the fight alive, I had to stay angry, at least long enough to win against the VA. I was back at war.

Chapter Eleven

ONCE HOME, I FOUND that with my wife at work, my daughter at school, and no more business, I had too much time on my hands. I was tired from my journey back to Vietnam. I needed peaceful thoughts and memories of a better time, a time full of happiness and anticipation for the future, a time to be with friends, laugh, and to find love.

I closed my eyes and leaned back into my recliner holding a letter I wrote my wife when I first arrived in country. I wrote Kathy of a new beginning, not of my time in Vietnam, but of our new life together. My love for her and my happy childhood still had me believing things would always be just fine.

Thinking of my youth put me into a relaxed mood and I drifted off to sleep, dreaming. It was 1960 and I was ten years old again.

✪ ✪ ✪

NEWLY FALLEN SNOW lay on our Long Island lawn that February night as I said goodbye. My dad, Phil senior, mom Nancy, brother Frank, sisters Luanne and Linda, our dog Cookie, and my dad's boyhood friend Mike piled into a '54 blue and white, two-tone Ford station wagon. I was happy to be heading to paradise, to Florida.

For months we waited for the trip and dreamed of a better life. It must have been a hard decision for two hard working young people of twenty-nine to pack it up with four kids and make a new start. I felt a sense of pride for my parents.

My dad worked construction and my mother did what ever she could, sometimes working as a supermarket cashier, other times as a waitress. It didn't matter. She did everything she could to ensure us kids never did without. Neither of my parents had been from wealthy families so it was important for them.

My dad worked hard and my mother was our strength. She never complained and she always found a way to make us feel better, no matter how bad things seemed to get. I tried to be that way with my daughter as well.

If my parents had a dream to go to Florida, then I was all for it. I dreamed of the beach, the palm trees, and of new adventures, but I still loved New York. I had plenty of friends back on the block and I would miss them. It didn't sink in for a ten-year-old. To me, our trip felt like a vacation.

As soon as we hit the North Carolina border we shed our winter clothes. As our car sped by, poor blacks worked the fields alongside cobbled-together shacks. The farm country turned to mountains, and then went flat again. When we hit Florida we all cheered.

"We're here, kids," Mom said.

"Yeah!" we responded in unison.

Just over the border we stopped for orange juice and watched an Indian wrestle an alligator. That night we stayed in a small motel. The water had an odor to it and didn't have the taste of New York water. When we took showers it smelled like a sewer pipe broke—sulfur water.

The next morning we were off again heading to Clearwater. We would be only a few short miles to the beautiful white sand beaches on the warm waters of the Gulf of Mexico. Before we settled in at another motel we headed to the beach. Palm trees lined the causeway to paradise.

All the kids ran down to the water, splashing in the foam. My parents beamed and held hands. Back then, moving to

Florida was something others only talked about. My parents had the courage to make the move and I'm glad they did.

It was hard at first—we didn't have a house so my dad found a trailer park in Clearwater. We needed two trailers, one for my dad's friend Mike, my brother Frank, and me, and another for my parents and two sisters. It was difficult but it was a start. Not quite the paradise yet.

Things didn't come easy and work was hard to find. In a couple of weeks dad found work in a new housing project about eighty miles away. Mom loved Clearwater so that's where we decided to settle. She also didn't want to stick us out in the middle of nowhere. Dad found us a house to rent and he worked laying concrete blocks in the hot Florida sun for about seventy-five dollars a week. He would drive home on the weekends and would always bring us something, usually a few fresh watermelons. Without much money we used the beach and drive-in movies for entertainment. That was all right with me.

Mike got an apartment but would visit all the time. Before we left the trailer one night, I noticed a deep red scar on his leg. He always walked with a limp and I knew he had been wounded in WWII.

"What happened?" I asked as he changed his pants.

"The Japs did it," he said while coughing from the cigarettes he always smoked.

"Does it hurt?"

"At times. They wanted to cut it off. I said hell no."

Mike was on disability from the VA. He worked part-time as a bartender and he had made pizzas in an Italian restaurant back home in New York. I loved it when he'd make homemade ones. When he moved I missed his cooking.

I also missed the way he'd take my brother and me hiking. We'd often walk through nearby woods to a large lake and a baseball field. We'd build a small fire and bake potatoes. Mike called them mickeys. He would march as if he was still in the Army and I'd laugh. I could tell he was proud he had served.

"You gotta march a lot in basic training," he'd say. "One, two, three, four!"

My brother and I would stand in back of him and try to get in step. At times would throw his hiking stick over his shoulder like a rifle.

"Hope you never have to experience war in your life time," he said.

I remembered the sight of his leg with that big deep red scar with half of his calf missing. War didn't sound pretty but most boys wanted to serve in some way. The movies showed adventure, excitement, and glory. They never showed you the trauma.

Mike passed on and I often thought of him. When I did I would smile at the way he marched with my brother and me. It must have been hard to live with the memory of what he went through, in WWII. Then again, maybe he had a chance to escape that memory at times when he went off with us kids. I hoped he did, anyway. We were protected as kids and never truly understood what war meant. We knew others went off to fight so we could be free. I never thought my time would come to fight for our country.

The years passed and I adjusted to new surroundings and friends. Boy Scouts, baseball, and the beach were all I needed. I had a glove autographed by Mickey Mantle and I never went anywhere without it. I hung it off the handlebars of my bike. My mom had saved her green stamps to get it for me. I dreamed of playing for the New York Yankees with my friend Lonnie. It was a good dream for two twelve-year-olds that played sandlot baseball every day. The crack of a good wooden bat against a ball headed out to far right field echoed in my head.

Suddenly the dream ended. I was back in combat, the

crack of AKs ricocheting in my ears as I sucked mud with Bill on the ground next to me. He popped off his M-79 while I ran at Viet Cong firing my M-16. An air strike pounded the whole area and shrapnel landed all around us. Our heads were in the ground so far that our fuckin' lips tasted the shitty mud of the 'Nam.

✪ ✪ ✪

I WOKE UP, SWEAT drenching me and the recliner. I tried to calm my racing heart. Fucking 'Nam had interrupted a damn good dream.

I couldn't return to the dream, but I could try to think back to that sweeter, easier time of my childhood. I could smell the orange blossoms as a bunch of neighborhood boys ran barefooted in cut-off shorts to the ball field. We raced toward the dugout of the little league field. We ran through the woods, across the railroad tracks, and jumped over a stream, then down a muddy trail and onto the smooth, well-kept grass of the diamond. To us it was heaven.

The crack of the wooden bat gave me an indescribable thrill. To hit a home run over some fence was the ultimate. Aluminum bats never felt the same. You need that *whomp* and high crack when you connected right. If you got that sound, you knew you had control. You were the one making it happen. If you heard that sound, you knew it was gone, over the chain link fence, maybe even into the lake.

I never made it to the Yankees, but that was all right. Lonnie moved about a year after we met. Years went by and I still watched the TV when a game came on to see if Lonnie somehow made it. I wondered what ever happened to him.

I joined Boy Scouts after Lonnie moved, but my interests changed two years later when I heard The Beatles blasting their new sounds on the Ed Sullivan show one Sunday night in 1964.

My blood boiled. The hard beat and electric chords of "She Loves You" drove teenagers wild. The voices of the Fab Four took control of the youth in the sixties. When the British music invasion started I found a hidden talent; I could sing. In high school I became the lead singer in a band, The Shadows Of Time, and found when I sang, I had control.

The summer after we graduated high school, most were getting ready for college, including all the guys in the band. I didn't want to go to college yet. I was having too much fun playing music, cruising the beach for girls, and hanging out with my high school friend Wally in my '57 Ford.

One night we had a gig for some college kids in an upper class neighborhood. We loaded my dad's old Chevy pickup and Wally's caddy and headed off to a party in Tarpon Springs, about twenty miles away. I was nervous playing for older kids but they made us feel comfortable. The talk of college and avoiding the draft was in the air.

"You guys goin' to school?" asked one guy, half-drunk on cheap beer.

We didn't drink much, so when others got drunk it was kind of funny.

"Yeah, I'm going to college," said our drummer Joe. He and I worked in the drugstore together.

The other members of the band all confirmed that college was in their plans as well.

I adjusted my microphone stand and didn't say a word.

A girl with beautiful eyes and a body that could stop a freight train walked up to me. "What about you?" she asked.

"Don't know yet," I said.

"Aren't you worried about Vietnam?"

"In a way. Whatever happens, happens, I guess."

She smiled at me and I thought she was thinking, "Man this guy's not afraid about Vietnam."

Or maybe she was thinking, "You dumb shit."

We set up our equipment and lights. This was our big shot to show them what we had. I never wanted to start until everyone was half-plastered. We cut the lights except for the colored lights we had shining on us. Bright colors of red, green and yellow reflected off our colorful silk Nauru jackets.

Lynn hit a chord on his Fender guitar, Joe banged out a beat, Ron strummed his guitar, Butch picked a bass note, Kim fingered the keyboards, and I hit the button on the strobe light. I removed the mike from its stand, and belted out the words to "Knock on Wood." Not too heavy, nice and easy.

I watched the crowd. The kids were digging it. As I saw their approval it made it easier. I glanced at the guys in the band; they felt it too. We were smiling and we were in control. I was singing and drunk college kids were all dancing. Wally gave me the sign everything was all right with the sound, and then he joined in with the other kids and started sneaking a few beers.

We went into another song, "Get Off Of My Cloud," by The Rolling Stones. Then "Devil With The Blue Dress." They went nuts when we launched into "I Feel Good." Guess they were shocked that a bunch of white guys could do James Brown. We slowed it down with "Don't Let The Sun Catch You Crying" and "My Girl."

We had a ball. We weren't thinking about Vietnam or school. It was what was happening at that very moment that really counted. All of us felt the same when we got to play. It was our way of releasing the stress of what was going on in the messed-up world. I'm glad I had the chance to feel the rush of standing in front of people singing my heart out.

I longed for that feeling again, but it was gone. I still liked to sing, but now mainly to myself or once in a while for a few friends. I forget the words and usually read them. The excitement isn't there anymore and my voice has lost some of its zest and power.

Maybe that's the way it's supposed to be after you experienced war. Not allowed to have fun anymore. I tried the band thing a couple of years after I returned home. It wasn't the same. I guess there's a time and place for everything.

The summer of '68 went fast. That was the summer I met my wife Kathy. It was the summer that changed the way I was to live the rest of my life.

"Wally, there are some girls coming down from up north," I said as we chowed down burgers in the Steak 'n Shake parking lot. "This girl I met said she's got cousins coming down from up north. One's our age—just graduated. Said we could meet them at the pier."

"Let's go down and see what's up," said Wally.

We started the car and before we pulled out this crazy guy drove through, revving his hot rod. He laughed and waved as his souped-up Barracuda passed by us.

"Look at that nut," I said.

"Nice car," said Wally.

"He's crazy. I've seen him a lot driving through here," I said. "Let's go man. We might have some girls waiting. Wipe your mouth; you've got ketchup on it," I said.

Wally smiled, raised his eyebrows, and wiped his face. Soon we were driving through the parking lot of the beach. We parked at the pier where kids were hanging around.

"Hi, remember me?" I said walking up to Mary.

"Oh yeah, Phil," she said, smiling back.

I was surprised she remembered. Her two cousins were there, Kathy—my age—and her little sister Rose—two years younger. Wally and I invited them down to a small teen club we were playing at that weekend. We were trying to drum up business for the new club that had just opened downtown.

That Friday night Wally had to go down and pick up a carload of kids. He didn't mind, especially because of the girls. When they came in I was already on stage and just finished

"Gimme Some Lovin'" by the Spencer Davis Group. They all clapped as they found seats.

"Hey man, we have a nice crowd," said Joe as he twirled his sticks.

"Yeah, what do we have, ten?" I said with a chuckle.

"At least we're playing," Joe said.

"Different than it was five years ago."

"You bet, buddy."

Back then Joe and I would walk the downtown streets peeking into nightclubs, trying to catch a glimpse of a live band. We'd stand on the side of the building pretending it was us up on stage. An all black band playing in the Crystal Lounge caught our souls like no other group we'd ever heard locally. The way they moved in step, their white suits, and the sounds of a horn they used was different. We liked the excitement.

"Man, we can do that!" I said.

We'd go see every band we could. One day we wound up in the bathroom at a civic center with a group called The Buckinghams. They had hits with "Kind of a Drag" and "Bus Stop." We talked and joked with them before they got on stage.

"Hey, we're in a band, too," I said to one, as I'm standing next to this guy taking a piss.

"What do you do?"

"Sing. He plays drums," I said, gesturing towards Joe.

"Keep it up, and thanks for coming out to see us."

"Yeah man, thank you," I said.

They smiled at us and left. Of course we became even bigger fans.

"Can you believe we met The Buckinghams?" Joe said.

"No, and nobody else will either," I said.

Toward the end of the summer most were off to school and the band was over. Kathy and I started to date more. I worked with my dad doing construction while Kathy worked at the grill in McCrory's drugstore. Things were changing fast as our love grew. I worried about the draft but I guess I thought it would just go away. I should have realized walking on the beach every night sure wasn't going to last forever.

For Kathy's birthday that year I paid off her engagement ring. The day I was going to give Kathy the ring I got greetings from Uncle Sam. I gave her the ring but didn't say a word about the draft notice until a few days later.

The party was over and the music seemed to die. The laughter and high school days were a thing of the past. It was a time that was good to my friends and me, and I'll always cherish it.

I felt so fortunate to have Kathy. She proved to be the best thing that would ever happen to me. Without her, it might have been hard to make it back. Many didn't have a wife back home. At times it made it hard, though. The "what ifs" again. What if I came home in a damn body bag, or lost a leg, arm, or everything? For a fun-loving guy of nineteen it was time to face the real world.

✪ ✪ ✪

THE PHONE RANG, jostling me out of my dream. I stumbled to the phone. "Hello."

"You're back, man?" Dan asked.

"Yeah. What's up?"

"Man, I'm fucked up," he said. Dan had that wired sound a guy had when he'd been thinking of Vietnam.

I knew the sound well.

Chapter Twelve

"WHAT'S WRONG, DAN?" I asked, leaning against the kitchen wall.

"Same old stuff. My nerves are shot," Dan said.

"Yeah, I know where you're coming from. I told you to call the Vet Center or to get down to the VA."

"But what if they stick me in that stress unit like they did you?"

"Well, you know that's what you need. I can't keep telling you what to do. You have to do it on your own."

I'd told Dan for months to get help. He'd gotten to where he could no longer handle the stress and work was far from his mind. His wife didn't know what to do either. She'd been with him before Vietnam. She'd told me of his nightmares and the anger. She loved him, but it hurt her to see what the war had done to her husband. With three kids it would be hard to just walk away from so many years together.

Dan and I had talked about Vietnam so many times, but this time our conversation seemed different. In the past Dan would only talk about the rush he felt in combat. Now he wished he had never left.

This time I could hear fear in his voice, begging for help. I thought he might even be in tears on the other end of the phone. He'd been dealing with Vietnam as long as I had, and he was an even bigger mess. This time, though, my time in the stress unit gave me some insight of what was going on, with him and so many other Vietnam veterans.

"I'm calling Joe and I'll have him call you, okay?" I said.

Dan didn't hesitate. "Yeah, maybe that would be good."

"Just don't do anything stupid."

"Maybe I'll blow my brains out."

"There you go again," I said. "Quit talking stupid shit."

"What?" He laughed, trying to cover his pain.

"You know what I mean," I said. "Just hold on a little longer. I'm going to get you some help."

I hung up and phoned Joe and told him about Dan.

"Does he have a gun?"

"He has a shit-load. He's ready for some damn revolution or next war. He wanted to go off to the Gulf War. He wanted me to go with him."

Joe laughed but knew how serious it was when a depressed vet had a weapon.

"Can you call him, please?" I asked.

"Yes, I will. Thanks."

I thanked him and gave him Dan's number.

I didn't need to be worrying about anyone else. I was fresh out of the hospital myself and had plenty on my mind. I was in pain and pissed off at the VA more now than ever. They had helped me open a can of beans that I thought might have been better off left closed. But not worrying about Dan wasn't an option. I had been with him too long not to.

✪ ✪ ✪

I REMEMBERED THE DAY I arrived in Vietnam. Dan, Dave, and I flew out to Oakland California. Sandy was already at Fort Hood, Texas. I felt good about that, but missed his ass. We became close in basic and AIT and we promised to stay in touch. Infantry was not in the cards for Sandy; his flat feet probably saved his life.

It was a long flight, stopping in Alaska, Hawaii, and then Guam. I remembered the plane banked and the pilot told us we would be landing soon in Vietnam. Our hearts went into our stomachs. We didn't talk; we didn't have to. All we had to do was to look at each other. We were scared. Who wouldn't be? All the things about Vietnam drilled into our heads. All the years hearing about the damn place. Before combat even started we had been on our way to becoming basket cases.

"So this is 'Nam?" I asked, glancing out the window. Large holes pocked the ground.

Shelling.

As the plane landed, I felt a chill curl up my spine. *Will I make it home?* I wondered. Even if I did, it would be a long time before I set foot on American soil again. The year stretched out unfathomably before me. The stewardess smiled at us as we disembarked. We all felt the warmth in her eyes for us. How many eyes had she looked at before mine? How many never came back?

The hot, humid air hit us hard, like we were walking into a damn oven. And the smell in the air was horrible. We later learned it stunk so badly from burning human waste, and I did a few details burning it myself to confirm it. We all heard the stories before, and so far they all were true. It wasn't a good sign.

They quickly ordered us to a bus that had protective mesh coverings over the windows. We walked past a large group of GIs sitting on the ground. They were in a hanger waiting for our plane—their freedom bird. They cheered us as we walked past.

I smiled and waved. I felt proud that I would take over where one of the poor bastards had left off. But they were going home, and my sorry butt would be the one on the line. Who was the poor bastard now?

Some wore deep sadness in their eyes. Some smiled. Some glazed over with a dead stare. Their skin had darkened—a tan like I had never seen before even though I lived in Florida. It looked like 'Nam did a number on the aging process.

"Are we gonna look like that when we leave?" I asked Dan.

"If we leave," he spat back.

Dave nodded and looked as if he was ready to turn and get back on the plane. He'd had a headache since Oakland.

They put us up in a barracks in Bien Hoa. The place was dirty, dusty and gloomy. The wooden barracks reminded me of something out of the old west. I thought it was a hellhole.

I would learn later on in my tour that it was not such a bad place to be stationed. The other places were the shit holes. Bien Hoa was pretty secure, only catching a mortar round now and then. That first night we were hit by mortar fire—our first taste of war. We learned early on that no place was safe.

After a few days we were sent to Tan An for a week of orientation.

A stocky sergeant with a Spanish accent barked out orders. "Forget what you learned in basic and AIT, about 'Nam! When you see your buddy's head blown off, fuck it man, don't mean nothin'; you must go on! They're only two kinds of people over here, people! The quick and the dead. Some of you FNGs won't make it back. You'll have your head stuck up your sorry asses. You know why? Because you didn't fuckin' listen!" He tried to make eye contact with each of us.

Man, this Ricky Ricardo look-alike was doing a number on us.

I was listening more than ever. I wanted to make it back and in one piece. So did Dan and Dave. Harvey had missed the plane, but he caught up with us. There was no way to escape the 'Nam.

We were finally separated. My friends went off to one battalion and I was sent to another. It was sad to leave them. They were the last piece of home I had with me. But this was a private ordeal. When the smoke cleared, you only had yourself.

"Cover your ass" was drilled into my head. I often thought of my drill sergeant in basic, Sergeant Martin.

"Keep your head down, you fuck-head," he said to me before I left Fort Benning, Georgia.

He rode us hard and I knew why. He had a job to do and not too much time to do it. He served in Vietnam and knew firsthand what we would be going through. There wasn't anyone more respected in the Army than a drill sergeant who had faced combat. Many times when I was in a tough situation I'd remember Sergeant Martin. I thought of his number twelve boot, ready to go up my ass if I didn't do right.

✪ ✪ ✪

EVERYTHING WAS COMING together, but in a mixed-up way. I was still so angry, but why? The VA denials? My wounds? My inability to work and the financial stress it put on my family? They were all really good reasons, but still, there was something else. Memories of Three-Six bounced around in my mind daily. Was it the memory of him getting wounded that angered me, or was it the fact that Three-Six had ordered me to run with him into that NVA base camp?

Maybe it was time to find him and talk to him. He had written me when I was still in 'Nam and I never wrote back. I always tried to avoid the issues. But maybe my ex-lieutenant had some answers for me.

I had an old letter he'd written me after he heard I was wounded. In the letter he mentioned he would probably have to stay in the hospital a whole year, rehabilitating from his wounds. He would need some plastic surgery on his nose where the bullet entered. He had also lost some use of his arm from nerve damage. He had offered his help with anything I needed and asked how I was being treated.

If only he knew how they were treating the guy who

helped save his life. But maybe after twenty years he could do something. Better late than never. Maybe he could write a letter explaining the action we were in to back my claim with the VA.

I took the address off of the envelope, a granite company up in Pennsylvania. I called the long distance operator and asked if there was still such a company. She connected me.

"Damn, that was easy," I said as the phone rang.

A woman answered.

"Hi, I'm looking for a John Raubar," I said. "I served with him in Vietnam."

"Yes, I know him," the woman answered. "I'm his aunt."

I couldn't believe how easy it was—after so many years to maybe reach him or one of his family members.

"Is he there?" I said.

"No. Leave me your name and number and I'll have him contact you. He doesn't live here."

I quickly got the impression she didn't want to give his number out. I said okay and left my number. The only thing I could do was wait to see if he'd call me.

I was on a roll and decided to call Bill out in Las Vegas. It had been too long. I got him on my first try.

"Hello," answered Bill.

"Hey buddy, it's Phil. What are you doing?"

He knew it was me right off. I told him about the hospital stay and what was going on in my life. He wasn't at all surprised that I was having problems with my wounds, the VA, and with memories of Vietnam. He also admitted that he too has had problems, not only with bad memories but with something else.

"Hey, remember when your faced swelled and they sent you to Japan?" Bill asked.

"How could I forget?"

"Well I get the same stuff. They don't know what it is. I

have to get some blood drained every so often. I was told maybe Agent Orange. They don't know."

This was no surprise to me. I saw it when I was in Japan. Others had it, but the government never admitted it could be from the stuff they sprayed all over us.

"Those bastards!" I growled.

"That Agent Orange is going to kill a lot of guys, you know that?" Bill said, anger rising in his voice.

"I hope not, Bill. What about the people who live in Vietnam? Ever hear anything about that?" I asked.

"No, they probably keep it from us."

"Do you ever hear from Chris any more?" I asked, knowing they grew up together and their families knew each other back in Ohio.

"My mom talked with his mom. He lives in Texas, somewhere outside of Dallas. Runs a rehab clinic or something."

"No kidding?" I said, surprised.

"Yeah, he was involved with a book back in the early 80s about 'Nam vets and PTSD. The book is called *Strangers at Home,* or something like that."

"I'll have to see if I can find it," I said.

"Yeah, he went to college on the GI bill. Got a degree, I guess."

This was great—if I could get a letter from Chris to support my claim it would help. We were close over there and he lived the ordeal with me. He knew how I suffered with the headaches.

"If you can, get me his number."

"Sure will. I'll write a letter for you too. I'll tell how you were wounded and not sent home. I couldn't believe it when I learned you where still in 'Nam."

I said thanks and we hung up. This time we said we would call each other more or try to see each other.

I was building evidence from old friends I served with. Dan had already said he would write a letter and Sandy also. If Chris and Three-Six could get in touch with me that would even be better—especially Three-Six. Joe at the Vet Center was working on a letter also.

Letters alone would not be enough—maybe to prove combat for PTSD—but not for the pain. I searched for an outside doctor. I needed a doctor who cared. Usually when they learned I was wounded, they'd dismiss me to the VA. I knew now that the VA alone was not the answer for my health care.

One VA doctor became enraged with me for seeking outside care and threatened not to treat me. I told him I needed answers and wasn't getting what I wanted from the VA.

He pissed me off enough that I complained about his verbal disrespect for a wounded veteran to the patient care department. The head of the complaint department, a wounded vet in a wheelchair, straightened him out.

I also refused to see that particular doctor again. I was refusing to have people walk over me like I had in the past. I realized it was now the Vietnam vet's chance to stand for what was right and what was deserved. The department was formed to take care of returning wounded veterans. It was time they started living up to their promise.

Chapter Thirteen

I WENT BACK TO Joe at the Vet Center. My stay at the stress unit had unleashed some deep feelings, and I needed more help.

"How's it going?" Joe asked.

"Look, I'm hurting. My stomach is all screwed up and when I eat it hurts. They did an upper GI but nothing showed. I'm gonna have to get some outside help. My wife set me up with an appointment with a doctor she's heard of. I'll try him for help."

"Okay...that might be a good idea."

"I have no choice, Joe. The VA sure the hell won't do anything."

Joe believed there was more than just pain from emotional stress, but the VA doctors wanted to blame all the pain on PTSD. To me it was just another excuse they used to avoid the issues, the biggest one being that my ass got shot up and no one wanted to do a thing to help me. I was entitled to a service connection for the wounds, as well as an increase for PTSD.

"Get with your service officer and follow up on your claim," said Joe.

"I was denied again, and I wasn't even out of the hospital yet."

Joe shook his head. "That's not uncommon. You'll be compensated back to when the claim went in, as soon as you are service connected."

"That doesn't help me now, you know? I'm so freakin' tired of fighting this shit. How in hell can they admit I'm suffering with PTDS and not service connect me?" I ranted. "Maybe it's all just a front, a way for the VA to get more funding every year. Sure, we can use these poor suckers again, like we did in 'Nam. This time we'll use 'em to keep our system alive. Big salaries for all jobs, new buildings, you name it."

Joe listened silently, taking notes as always.

"One time I asked to use the new CAT scan. Know what the doctor said? He said, 'Hell, just because we have a new million dollar machine, doesn't mean anybody can use it.'"

"Someone said that to you?" Joe asked.

"Yeah, I know his name. You want to know?"

"No, that's all right."

"What good would it do me anyhow? The guy is probably retired now, sitting on his ass enjoying his pension!"

"You have to learn how to calm down," Joe said. "Let me tell you a story."

I respected Joe. I knew he cared a lot for vets because he was one of us. He also hurt from the horrors of war. Although he wasn't a combat troop, guilt consumed him. Each day he watched caskets being lined up to be returned to their loved ones. I listened.

"For a long time I worked with a guy I knew had a decent rating coming to him," Joe said. His voice was low and dark. "One day he was finally granted a proper rating. But it was too late."

"Why's that?" I said.

"He killed himself."

"Oh man, Joe. That must have been hard on you."

"He shot himself before he had possession of the check for retroactive compensation. His family couldn't get the check so they couldn't pay their debts."

I hung my head. "It's harder on the ones left behind," I said.

"You bet," Joe said. "Never give up. Promise me that?"

"I won't."

I knew I had a commitment to my family. My wife stuck by me all through the war, and now with my screwed up life. It hurt me because I was bringing her back to a time we both thought was behind us. Sooner or later, the trauma of war had to come back to haunt me. I had a lot to deal with, both physically and mentally. It was hard to separate the two.

"You know Phil, I can see the stress. Can you imagine a cup full of water? Your cup is overflowing. You can't add anymore. I also honestly feel you'll never return to work again," said Joe.

I felt the same but never admitted it to myself. A man must sometimes face the truth, no matter how much it hurts.

"I want you to start my group on Thursday nights. Can you do that?"

"Yeah, I guess. What kind of guys are in this group?"

"All right guys. Some I've worked with a while, some new like you. Don't worry, you'll fit in."

"I'll be there. What about Dan?"

"Yeah, he's been in a few times to see me. He's going to be a hard one to work with because he's got a lot of anger. He's not in the group yet. I think he should go through the stress unit first."

I thought the same thing, but part of me feared it might make him worse.

"Well, see ya Thursday," I said.

We shook hands and I was on my way again. Little did I know what impact my Thursday nights at the Vet Center would have on me over the next three years. The intense emotions never relented. As I'd listen to others, I'd relate their situations to my own. I was truly obsessed with getting my claim through. I wanted to find peace and it didn't seem like an easy thing to do.

I still had appointments with the audio department at the VA. Stress management was something that I tried but wouldn't allow myself to surrender to. I wanted to stay angry, at war. Finding an outside doctor would not be easy either because of the wounds. My hands were worse also. The VA would only give me Motrin for the pain. I was popping about 3000 milligrams a day.

"My stomach hurts. Can I take all these?" I asked once.

"Oh yeah, just eat first," said the doctor.

I followed up with the appointment my wife made with a doctor named Nelson Smith. I was lucky he was taking new patients.

Only a week after making the appointment, I was in his office telling him what was going on. I even mentioned the stress unit and my struggle with the VA. He was not surprised.

"I interned at the VA," he said.

He ordered blood tests, x-rays, a urine test, and he did a full exam. I already knew I had arthritis in my wound area, but the doctor also discovered blood in my urine. He was also very concerned with the burning in my chest.

He wanted me to see an urologist. My prostate gland was enlarged. A test I had been given put me in the hospital with complications. I thought I'd die because I couldn't urinate and my kidneys started to shut down. The pain was unbearable.

After that incident I wanted to be left alone for a while. Dr. Smith ordered some pills for my stomach which I took until my next visit a few months later. He told me to quit the Motrin, so I did, but I still needed Tylenol and some aspirin for pain. He put me on medicine for hypercholesterolemia and hypertriglyceridemia, specialized cholesterol-related diseases.

My treatment by Dr. Smith was radically different than my treatment at the VA. The VA knew my cholesterol levels were dangerously high, but no medical treatment was ever ordered. I had told them I was having problems urinating throughout the night. I had been told my prostate was enlarged but nothing was done. They totally disregarded the blood in my urine. I was told that I was doing fine, "for my age."

I learned a lot of guys exposed to Agent Orange had prostate problems and that worried me. The more I heard about Agent Orange the more it upset me. How could I trust the government anymore, especially with the way I was being neglected?

I asked for the test that proved exposure to Agent Orange offered by the VA. The test consisted of questions and a blood test. The results read "Not exposed."

From what I figured, we all were exposed. We lay on the banks of the muddy delta right after they sprayed the defoliant. We walked into burnt areas all the time after planes flew over our heads dropping the chemical all over. The government admitted that Agent Orange could be a contributing factor in stress disorders, headaches, skin problems, and numbness in the hands and feet. The solution was easy—give a half-ass test then say you're all right, and then they're off the hook.

I had to take control of my own life. I couldn't rely on the government to take care of my medical needs. Outside doctors helped me get some answers, and armed with the information they gave me, the VA could be of more help.

I still had one big problem. I discovered that if you were being treated for pain from a wound the VA automatically figured you were complaining for more compensation and tried to brush you off. I'd seen vets get top-notch treatment when it had to do with something they wouldn't be getting any money for. A lot of VA doctors would deny it, but I'd seen it too many times.

I phoned the VA and made an appointment to see my 201 file. I had been told I had the right to look through my records and ask for anything out of them. They scheduled me several months down the road but I didn't care. I wanted to put together a claim this time that was backed by good hard evidence. There had to be something in my file they weren't considering, maybe even hiding. Why was I always denied?

A few months later, another decision came through. This time I was service connected for PTSD but with no addition to my rating of sixty percent. I was paid at the one-hundred-percent rate for the two months I stayed in the hospital. I had been out of the hospital for quite some time, but the money helped. Christmas was on the way and we had nothing—we were at each other's throats. My nerves were shot and my wife worked her ass off at a bakery for five dollars an hour.

It got to where I didn't want to talk on the phone. I avoided people. They added stress. I usually kept the machine on, but one day I had forgotten and picked up the phone after a few rings.

"Is this Phil?" the caller asked.

"Yes."

"This is John." He paused. "Three-Six."

I swallowed hard. "How are you, John?"

"Sorry it took so long to get to phone you. I just got the message. I've been going through a divorce. Long story."

We talked about the day he got injured. He didn't remember much. "I remember running into the base camp and shooting at the running NVA. Then I got hit. Everything else is kind of blurry."

I told him how hard it was to get a dust-off.

"You're kidding me."

"I wish I was. It still makes me nervous just thinking about it. I got hit later that night."

We went through all the details of the battle over the phone. My heart started racing again. The fear surged up, and I remembered firing at those VC like I was in a carnival shooting gallery.

"How are you feeling?" Three-Six asked.

"To tell the truth, I've been having a rough time lately. I have a claim in with the VA for wounds and PTSD," I said.

He was quiet. He too had his share of medical problems.

"My arm is screwed up from the bullet. Sometimes I can't lift a thing," he said. He was a building contractor like me, but was now going to school to be a nurse.

"Have you tried help from the VA?" I asked.

"The hell with them. I get forty percent if I can work. I'd rather not mess with them."

It was fine that Three-Six wanted to work if he could, but I was hurting too much. There was no way I'd be able to work again.

"Can I do anything for you?" asked Three-Six.

"Well, maybe write a letter so I can turn it in with my claim."

"Sure, I'll write the President."

"Yeah, right." I laughed.

After a half hour conversation we said our goodbyes. We exchanged addresses and he told me he wanted to come down to Florida. He just got remarried and Florida might be nice for a fresh start.

It was hard to talk to him after so many years. The thought of seeing him made me nervous. The last picture in my mind of him was with a bullet between his eyes; it never left my mind.

Contacting my lieutenant would give me something to talk about in the group. I had started to get comfortable talking in the sessions so I thought they would find it interesting. So would Joe.

One of the guys in the group, John, was having a rough time. He was out of SRU and his problems were getting worse. His claim was messed up worse than mine.

"I have this weird nightmare," he said over the phone one day. "I'm getting ready for an operation by some doctors. I open my eyes and a gook looming over me. Just his shadow. I can't see him, but I could see the shape of his damn hat. I woke up in a cold sweat. I can't get the dream out of my head."

"I know what you mean," I said. "You get this thought in your head and it drives you nuts. For me, it's when I was wounded. Maybe that's you too."

"I guess so. It pisses me off. Even when I'm awake the dream haunts me."

John opened up in group one day, explaining what had happened to him soon after he arrived in country. He served with the marines as a grunt. After a battle there were many GIs lying around dead. The sight still haunted the hell out of him. But it got worse. He was ordered to do a detail which sickened him.

"Put bodies together, everyone gets a head, two arms and two legs," ordered his platoon leader. "Fuck it if it don't match!"

What a memory to have been carrying around for so many years. Soon after that he was involved in a ground attack by NVA and he was wounded. He got shrapnel in his back and knees, and his hand was just hanging by a damn hair.

"We have to cut it off," they told him.

"Fuck you man! You're not cutting it off!"

Doctors saved the hand but it was hard to use now. At least he made them keep it. He wound up in a hospital for a long period of time and had a real bad attitude about everything. He punched a guy while he was processing out—his records got screwed over and he got out with jack shit. He only had a ten percent rating, and like myself, was in battle with the VA. After being married four times, he figured he had a problem.

No shit he had a problem. When it started to thunder, his ass was in a closet.

John was angry a lot. He'd disagree with other vets, just to argue. At times he actually looked for someone to piss him off.

Jim, another member I talked to a lot, was also dealing

with stress from the war. Jim served with the Army in the 4th Division. A major battle in Dak To still haunted him. He was involved in the battle of Hill 875 on Thanksgiving Day, 1967. Many lost their lives trying to take that damn hill.

"Why man? Just to give it back?" Jim said while hanging his head. His sad eyes told it all—the sleepless nights, the anguish. After twenty years with a building supply company he quit. The stress was just too much. He had been attending the Vet Center but didn't tell his boss because he was ashamed.

One day on the job a guy pulled up covered with blood. He got hurt working off a truck. Jim flashed back. He saw the 'Nam battle scenes again. He had only been in country a few days when he was wounded in an ambush. As he lay in the medivac chopper, the door gunner noticed his new fatigues.

"How long you been here, man?" he asked.

"Only a few days."

"You ain't gonna make it. What do you have, another three hundred and a wake-up?"

The thought stayed with him the remainder of the year— twelve months in the field. It didn't seem right to make someone stay out that damn long. It could have been different, and it might have made a difference if some didn't have to endure so many consecutive months in the bush.

The group was often asked, "If you were in charge, what would you do different?" No one ever answered because no one knew, not for sure.

But Joe knew I had this bitter taste about the way I ran into the NVA camp. He knew I had made contact over the phone with the man who ordered me to run in. He looked at me.

"Phil, what would you do different?"

My face flushed. "My ass probably wouldn't have ran into that camp like an asshole," I said.

"Are you mad at your lieutenant?"

"I don't know."

I thought about it. I guessed I was. Was it time to forgive him? Was this another lost answer to one of many questions? I think it was, and Joe knew it. We all didn't like to take orders from anyone. I knew I didn't. I'll make my own decisions, thank you. If I fucked up then it was my fault.

We all agreed it was a big problem dealing with some officers who didn't have much more training than we did. A little OCS, Officers Candidate School, and you're in charge of men's lives. The way I looked at it was you didn't know shit about war until you got your ass shot at or saw your first dead GI. Then you'd know how you'd react and could actually be responsible for other men's lives. It was a big job and it weighed heavily those young officers. Some even got fragged, killed by their own men, because they fucked up. Was that right? No, but it was war. Our minds were changed to survive the ordeal.

As I looked at each hurting man in the group I wondered, *But did we really survive?*

I remembered after I was wounded I was assigned to a unit that worked security around the base perimeter. When I walked into the mess hall one day, I noticed a man sitting alone. Not knowing anyone, I invited myself to sit with him.

"Hi. Can I sit here?" I asked.

He nodded without looking up from his plate. He was a muscular man with a scar down the left side of his cheek. He looked to be an Indian with his dark eyes, hair and complexion. As I took my seat, others turned to look at us.

"My name is Phil. New here."

"I'm Tom. Sorry, I don't talk much."

"Oh, no problem."

"How long ya been here?" I asked.

"Long enough. This is my third tour."

"Three tours!"

"Long story," he said.

I later learned Tom came over with a friend on his first tour. While on a recon mission, his hometown friend was captured by the VC. The next day his body was found hanging from a tree, skinned. Tom was never the same again. He signed up for another tour to avenge the murder of his friend.

During his second tour, Tom fell in love with a girl working at a PX. She was a beautiful half-French, half-Vietnamese girl who also fell in love with Tom. With the help of the girl he loved, Tom was able to accept some of the pain that was caused by his friend's death. They made plans to marry so the girl could come home with him to the States.

Only days before they were to leave, a mortar attack ended Tom's dreams. The PX was blown up, and so was Tom's only true love.

Tom felt worthless and had no desire to return home. Against the advice of his company's officers, he signed on for another tour. He got the name Chief Tommy Three Tour. Rumor had it he had more gook ears than I had days left in country.

As time went on, I became close to Tommy. He would tell me his thoughts on life and war.

"Ya know, maybe I should have gone home," he said as we drank a beer together one night. "I've had enough of war, more than most."

"What will ya do when you get back, Tom?"

"Who knows? Always thought this was home and the Army would be my life. But now I know it's time to move on."

I sat there watching a hardened man crumble right in front of me. His callused hands trembled as he raised his beer for the last gulp. His head went back and I glanced down to the long Bowie knife attached to his belt.

How many ears had been cut off by that knife?

I felt for this hurting man I'd come to know only as a gentle person. I didn't feel for the ones he had cut up.

"One more beer and I'm gone, buddy."

"Where ya going, Tom?"

"Recon. Wanna go?"

"No, man. Can't handle that shit anymore."

"Sure could use a good RTO. The lieutenant told me to ask ya."

"No, that's all right. Maybe another time."

Tommy smiled and grabbed another beer, something I hardly ever saw him do.

"If you're going out you shouldn't drink anymore, Tom."

"What the hell. Maybe it will calm my nerves. Feeling kind of mellow right now. Fuck it. Don't worry. Never know— this might be my last mission."

We both looked at each other and didn't say a word. War had already damaged our souls beyond repair.

"Gotta go. See ya tomorrow. Keep looking at those stars, Phil. One of 'em is yours. You have something to go home to. You are one lucky guy."

"I sure am. And hey—" I said seriously, grabbing his hand. "—you watch your ass and be careful, will you? Remember, you're going home soon."

Tom smiled and said, "Yeah, I'm finally going home. I feel it's time."

We shook hands and Tom sauntered away.

That was the last time I ever saw him.

His recon squad walked into an ambush. Tom was caught alive and tortured by the VC. He died the way he himself had treated the dead. He had been a causality of war even before he was killed.

Chapter Fourteen

ISOLATION WAS SOMETHING I was getting used to. Hunting through the papers and medical records I had to sort through, memories of Vietnam continued to plague me.

Isolation wasn't the only problem—trying to get a good night's sleep since Vietnam was a terrible challenge. But that was no longer a puzzle. Joe had told me that many combat veterans had altered sleep patterns. It might take years for normal sleep patterns to be restored, or they might never get back to normal. What good was someone who only got a few hours a night?

"Someone from the General Accounting Office in Washington is coming down," Joe said one day. "They want to check things out, hear any complaints the vets might have. Would you like to attend a group on that day? I'm asking a few out off each group."

"I'll come," I said. "Hope I don't get off on some sore subject, like how the rating process has screwed me over."

Joe gave me a grin.

The next week I listened as a polite lady from Washington asked the questions. She took notes as veterans said what was on their minds. Most mentioned not getting their disability ratings increased, or their medical needs not being met.

I was the only one not saying a word. I was also one of a few actually wounded in action. I wanted to talk, but couldn't. I figured it wouldn't do any good anyhow.

One guy whined about some petty thing he'd been dealing with. I sat there trying to listen with one of my famous ongoing migraines. My chest burned, my ears rang, and the PTSD symptoms were in high gear.

"Anyone have anything else to say?" the woman from Washington asked.

"Yeah, I do," I blurted out. "I haven't worked now in over a year because I hurt all the time." I surprised myself. My mouth was ahead of my brain. I was off and running and my temper was getting the best of me. I felt control slipping from me and it scared me.

"I went into the hospital for two months," I continued. "Nothing was done for my pain, and only now have I been diagnosed with this stress bullshit, with no rating!"

Joe had been out of the room, but he quickly ran in when he heard my voice getting louder. He closed the doors behind him.

I took one look at him and calmed down. Most in the room were uneasy but agreed with what I was saying. I blasted out about mistreatment, not only to me, but other Vietnam veterans. I told how the rating board didn't look at all the evidence. After about ten minutes of directing my anger toward the system I said, "That's all, for now."

The veterans in the room erupted in supportive applause.

My head was pounding with the excruciating headache— the same headache for twenty-three years, every week. Ten percent for a head wound with a three-inch long scar along my left ear, just under the hairline.

It was not just the scar. What about the arthritis that had developed in my neck, the shrapnel never removed, the ringing in the ears that could at times drive me nuts? None of it seemed to matter. It didn't matter because those that could make a difference didn't care. It didn't involve them so they didn't have a clue.

The meeting broke and I went in to talk with Joe.

"Sorry I went off," I said.

"You have every right to get mad," said Joe.

For months I had been keeping a journal at Joe's request. Every week Joe would read what I had written. I knew writing down my feelings might be a way to help myself. It hadn't helped that day, though.

But over time I did improve. And the more I healed, the more I felt driven to build the strongest case possible. I ordered action reports from Washington. The action reports showed when I was wounded and the action our unit was involved in. The reports even showed when we took prisoners.

The reports never mentioned names of the soldiers who caught the action. We were just numbers. I received no credit for single-handedly catching two VC in Cambodia. I had been left alone in some damn heavily-occupied NVA war zone. It was a screw-up and I was the one being screwed.

But now I had a little better understanding of it all. Somehow I knew I needed stressful events to prepare myself for worse stress later in life. Without the little incidents along the way, I wouldn't have a story. Each event played an important part in my one-year tour of Vietnam.

✪ ✪ ✪

ONE DAY WE WALKED into an abandoned Cambodian village. The cooking fires were still hot and coals from the wood could have easily cooked one of those ducks the villagers always had in a pot. This time, maybe *we* were the damn ducks.

It was a fairly large village with two-story huts made from bamboo. They amazed me. The village houses in Cambodia seemed to be better than the ones in Vietnam. The people in Cambodia had a different culture. Cambodians had a darker skin and looked like they ate better—the ones I saw anyway. All the same, back then a gook was a damn gook.

I had strange vibes about the empty village. We filled canteens from fifty-gallon drums, something that we later realized was dumb. Stupid GI. For some reason everybody got up and left this village.

We walked through each house searching for evidence of NVA. I took notice of a calendar hanging on a bamboo wall in a sleeping area. Yesterday had been marked off, so I figured everyone was still there the day before. The last time we had walked through a village, the people just stood there looking at us with a stare that cut right through you.

"Look man!" yelled Preacher. A large black man from Mississippi, he wasn't really a preacher, but he read the Bible constantly and we figured he was the guy closest to God.

"A bunker!" shouted Preacher again.

Quickly we all hovered around a two-foot diameter hole in the ground. We had our weapons pointed into the hole. We were ready for a mad minute. That's when you release all your frustrations; unload about five or six magazines of ammo.

"Who wants to go down?" asked Three-Six.

"Yeah right," I said. "Blow it up. I ain't goin' down. I'm married."

"Fuck you, I ain't," said Jerry.

"May the Lord be with ya, Three-Six," Preacher said, walking backwards from the bunker. "May he give you strength as you go down there." With eight months in country, Preacher didn't take chances. He was also skilled as a point man but during our Cambodian mission he was walking as a regular rifleman. We wanted to protect our preacher as he was winding down his tour.

Bill shook his head in disbelief. Did Three-Six really expect someone to volunteer?

We all stepped back.

"I'll go," said Three-Six.

"Go ahead," I said. "You're crazy."

"I can't believe you just don't blow it up," Bill said.

"Step back," Jerry said. "Let him go." He gave me a nod to move away.

Three-Six took his 45 pistol and a flashlight and headed down the hole. I guess someone had to do it and he figured he shouldn't ask anyone to do something he wouldn't do first. That's one thing I have to say; he looked out for his men the best he could.

We were lucky—no enemy and plenty of supplies. Tons of rice, clothing, and even some weapons—a few crossbows, which I had always feared getting shot by.

Our lieutenant was like a kid who just raided the cookie jar. We joked and laughed, but I still had the feeling the enemy was still close, closer than I ever felt before.

"Phil, stay here with the radio. Start pulling these supplies out to the road. Call the captain and have the stuff picked up. I'll take the squad down that trail." Three-Six pointed to a skinny path that went off into some deep green brush.

Three-Six and the rest of the squad left and I was standing there like an orphan. Not liking the situation, but not thinking much about it, I took off the radio and set it down with my M-16. I started dragging the heavy bags of rice to the road about fifty feet away. After a few trips back and forth, I noticed movement out of the corner of my eye. Realizing my M-16 was not in reach, my heart skipped a beat. Helpless. I was totally helpless.

I made a mad dash for the M-16. I didn't look over to see what was moving because I didn't want whoever it was to know I saw them.

I ran around one of the huts and saw two men standing there in black shorts and worn-out, dirty white T-shirts. They turned their heads.

"Hands up!" I yelled, nervously pointing my M-16 at them. My finger was tight on the trigger. I was ready to unload at that second.

Their hands went up and their eyes widened. I was in charge of the situation. Shit, it was about time I had control over something.

I ordered them to move by pointing my M-16 in the direction of the radio. I ordered them to lie down on their stomachs, face down, with their hands in back of them.

They obeyed my every command. It was a good, in-control type feeling. A rush coursed through my body. It was unlike anything I had ever experienced before.

I grabbed the horn and yelled for Three-Six. "Get the hell back! I have two gooks, man."

"Be there right away. Three-Six out."

"You guys just lay right here," I said to my prisoners. "Ya scared the shit out of me."

They grinned, not understanding a word I said. They didn't look like much of a threat, but I didn't want to take any chances. Why were they there snooping around when everyone else had left? I figured they were doing some sort of recon for the NVA.

✪ ✪ ✪

WHEN I TOLD JOE about that day, he shook his head. "Did you get a medal for that?" he asked.

"What? A dumb shit medal?" I laughed. "We never got medals for much of anything. I think to get a medal you needed to save someone under fire."

"Maybe, but some have received medals for doing far less things than you have described to me," said Joe.

I never thought much about the medals. Years later, I thought they would have been nice for my kids or grandkids.

"I'm really having a hard time with this lately, Joe. You see how I blew up with the GAO lady. At home I've been jumping down everybody's throat. I feel like I'm losing control. I'm sick of all the denials and the system."

"Look, if you need a time out, maybe you should go into the hospital for a few days."

I didn't want to go into the hospital again for PTSD. I had a claim pending and I thought they would think I was trying to create more support for my case.

Joe didn't relent. "If you need to go to the hospital, I'll write a note. You take it with you and should have no problem getting admitted."

The headaches were coming more frequently, without even a single day in between for relief. When my weekly meeting at the Vet Center rolled around, I was in no shape to drive the twenty miles to the meeting. I called just before six o'clock.

"I can't make it tonight. I have a very bad headache," I said.

"No problem," said the receptionist.

"Just tell Joe why I can't come down."

"I'll tell him. Your name is Phil?"

"Yeah, he'll know who I am."

A large rainstorm was heading our way and the gloom matched my mood. As the thunder rumbled in the darkened sky, my head hurt worse. The sounds of thunder and the cracking of lightning have always reminded me of my many nights spent in the jungle. I could still feel the cold rain pounding down on me and my comrades without mercy.

I looked forward to the meetings, but with a migraine they were hard to handle. Even so, I should have gone.

My wife and daughter had an argument over something mundane like homework. Their voices just got louder and louder. Combined with the thunder, I found myself on the edge.

"Keep it down, will you?" I yelled. "I've got a damn

headache."

"You've always got a headache," shouted Kathy.

My situation was taking a toll on my wife—my health, the denials, not working. A year had passed since my hospital stay and things weren't really all that better.

I refused to give in but wondered if my wife could endure the struggle much longer. I was determined to handle it alone if I had to, just so she wouldn't have to suffer along with me.

Our marriage was being tested to the limits. I hated bringing her back to Vietnam with me, and that's just what I did. She watched me change and she felt for me. It just wasn't fair.

The isolation was also taking its toll on her. I only talked with other vets in the same situation and I didn't want to go anywhere. I hated to drive, and when I did, my rage came out. I'd cuss out any guy who cut me off, and then speed up to try to catch him. I was not a fun person to be around.

"You're crazy!" Kathy screamed. "That hospital made you worse."

"Thanks a lot," I said, shooting her a nasty look.

"Look in the mirror and see what you've become," she said. "See what I see. That angry man is not my Phil."

The thunder crashed and I jumped. "I've gotta get the hell out of here!" I shouted.

"You can't drive in this. You'd better not go," Kathy said with tears in her eyes.

My daughter wailed as I slammed the door to the garage. My old truck would get me the hell out of there. I had no idea where I was going, but I found myself heading towards the VA hospital. It was almost as if the truck was on automatic pilot.

The rain was hard and the streets were getting flooded.

"Damn it!" I cried out. I kept driving. The song "Who'll Stop The Rain" by Credence Clearwater was on the radio.

Another song: "Run Through The Jungle." I kept hitting

the buttons on the radio. "Stormy" by The Classics Four.

Kathy and I loved that song. While I was in basic, Kathy told me she loved it. Tears poured down my face as I drove in the rain. Maybe if I had gone to the meeting this wouldn't have happened. But no, something had to pop sooner or later.

I was almost to the entrance of the hospital when I came to a stop.

"Fuck you!" I yelled at the hospital building.

I hated what was happening to me. I held them responsible for what was going on. It wasn't all the hospital's fault, but much of it was, because I couldn't get an answer for the pain. The pain was driving me nuts.

"You bastards!" I yelled again. "I won't even give you the privilege of taking me in!"

I pulled away, confused. I wanted to get drunk but only had a couple of bucks in my pocket. Two bucks wouldn't get me much in a bar. I could get in a fight, though. Couldn't drink with a headache, and why should I take my anger and frustrations out on some poor soul sitting in a bar?

I continued to drive aimlessly through the pouring rain. Twenty minutes later, I found myself parked in front of my old high school.

"Old Clearwater High," I said softy. It was just me in the dark in my truck as it rained like hell. "What happened, man?" I said.

I looked at the school, wanting comfort from a time I missed and loved. A time when I was a happy kid. I looked over to the front of the school and saw the flagpole and the war memorial for those who had died in battle.

"The hell with the rain," I said, stepping out of the truck. I wanted to talk to the names on the memorial. I never walked up to the monument and it was about time I did. I don't think anybody paid it much mind. It seemed as though it was always just there. I wondered if anyone from our class ever really looked at it. If they did, it probably was a veteran.

Rain plastered my clothes to my skin as lightning struck all around me. I touched the stone monument but couldn't read the names in the darkness.

"Thanks, guys," I said. "I'm sorry."

I turned and ran across the street to a pay phone and called Joe.

"Hello, is Joe there?"

"Yeah, hold on."

"Joe, it's Phil. I blew up."

"Where are you?" Joe asked. He had been in the middle of the Thursday night meeting I was supposed to be at, and left it to help me.

"In front of my old school in Clearwater."

"What happened, Phil?"

I told Joe that I just got mad about things and my head was hurting.

"Come down here."

"No, it's too far. And it's raining cats and dogs here," I said.

"Go to the hospital with that letter I gave you."

"I can't go there with those assholes. I'll be all right. I'll go home."

"Look, call me tomorrow. I'm concerned about you."

"Yeah, thanks. I'll see ya," I said.

I calmed down as I walked back to the truck. The water ran down my neck, inside of my shirt, to the crack of my ass. It didn't matter. I'd been wet before and nobody cared. Sleeping in mud up to your neck in the swamps was a lot worse than this.

What the hell did all of this prove? Shit, that's what. Who did I hurt? The ones I loved the most.

I made it home and my wife and daughter were already in bed. I peeked in and saw my little girl, my pride and joy, sleeping peacefully.

My wife woke up. "You okay?" she asked.

"Yeah, I'm sorry. I'll try to control my self."

"You have to call Dr. Smith again and tell him you still have the pain."

"Okay, go to sleep. I gotta sit up some."

"Okay, but come to bed soon. You need some sleep."

I walked to the rear of the house to the family room. I glanced at my old guitar standing by the fireplace. I picked it up, sat down in my recliner, and started to strum while thinking of Bunny.

"Hardly play anymore, Bunny," I said as I softly stroked a G chord, then A, then D. I seemed to just play chords, not songs, as if I was searching for some lost melody.

"I wish I had the ten-dollar flat-top guitar you gave me, buddy," I whispered.

Someone stole Bunny's guitar from me when I was sent to Japan. Someone had stolen a piece of a memory from me. A friend was dead, and I couldn't remember what his face looked like.

I put the guitar down and turned on the TV. I watched scenes from the Gulf War. Some vets were complaining about being sick.

"The shit they sprayed!" I yelled. "We never finished the job. Should have killed that bastard!"

I was mad but nothing sickened me more than watching a young marine's body being dragged through the streets of Somalia. I cried in disbelief as I watched it on the TV. When it came on the news again I had to leave the room. I was, like any good American, deeply disturbed. I took it as a personal slap in the face to all Americans.

Vietnam had made me very bitter about Americans dying for countries that wouldn't help themselves. They'd kill their own kind other over anything. The strong would always take from the weak, just like the government continued to take from me and my fellow veterans. It made me sick.

Chapter Fifteen

WITH EACH DENIAL from the VA, came more anger. What were they doing? What other evidence could I give them? I had a doctor's report turned in from their own. Every week I'd phone my service rep who worked for the Disabled American Veterans.

"This should do it," she'd say. "I'll hand walk this new report in myself." She tried, but the point wasn't getting across. Then they changed service reps on me and I had to start all over.

I finally got an appointment to go downtown to the regional office where I could look through my file.

I was called into a small room where a VA worker greeted me with a six-inch thick folder—my records dating from when I had been drafted. "You can take as long as you like and I'll give you copies of anything," said the polite man.

I tried to explain what I'd been going through with the rating system, and he nodded. He'd obviously been that route before.

I opened the folder. I couldn't believe it. My eyes started to water. The very first page was to President Clinton from my lieutenant. *Three-Six did write him, son of a gun*, I thought.

I read Three-Six's letter. "I do owe a debt of personal gratitude to this man, as it was he who was at my side when I received a gunshot wound to the head twenty-two years ago," he wrote. "It is likely I owe my life to this fellow's courage and assistance. The efforts of your office would be greatly appreciated." He also mentioned how some records were lost in fires in Vietnam and at the National Records Center in St. Louis.

"Look, a letter to the President," I said to the VA worker.

He smiled. "I can have the whole file sent to you, if you'd like," he offered.

"That would be great. Thanks."

When my file arrived I poured over it. The more I read, the angrier I became. The rating board had access to the Vet Center reports, letters from comrades, my mother and endless doctor's reports, but "denied" was the only word they knew how to write.

I became deeply disturbed and hurt when they would consistently deny a shrapnel wound to my right shoulder. Numerous x-rays showed a fragment still remaining. There was a hospital report from Vietnam in my folder showing the shrapnel wound. It was dated January 25, 1971. Also, reports dated September 30, 1993, November 27, 1991, and May 14, 1993 showed Department of Veteran Affairs x-rays. Each report stated fragment wounds. Outside doctor's reports showed both shoulders with shrapnel. Then on October 8, 1993 I was sent a decision stating they denied a service connection for right shoulder wound.

I guess I should have checked the city records or my high school to see when we might have came under a mortar attack in Clearwater, Florida.

It went on and on—continuous medical reports showed I was suffering with angioneurotic edema while in Vietnam and also at Fort Hood, Texas. Records showed me being sent to Camp Zama, Japan because of the swelling, but I went untreated until I made it to a civilian doctor while on leave. He said I should be discharged with the condition. My father-in-law had it during WWII. He only served one month, swelled up, and received a discharge.

On November 18, 1992, the St Petersburg Times printed

an article from Washington.

"The Pentagon has advised U.S. military personal not to wear old wool uniforms that might contain hazardous DDT. Armed Forces and civilians should not use surplus blankets treated with the pesticide. The statement followed the department's confirmation Monday that it manufactured and distributed seven million uniforms and one-point-five million blankets made from the wool treated with a banned chemical. Many of the military blankets have been given to homeless people and disaster victims worldwide since 1987, even though the Environment Protection Agency ban on cancer-causing DDT went in effect twenty years ago. Spokesman Pete Williams said in mid-1940s, the U.S. Military treated its wool cloth with DDT to protect from moths and other insects. He said blankets made without DDT treated wool are stamped with the letters "U.S.".".

I had turned in the article because doctors told me it was possible I was having a reaction to DDT used in and around the area where I had been. I even found a report in my file that stated I had a job in Vietnam spraying DDT.

Records also showed me complaining back on January 18, 1984 of a burning feeling in my back under the wound and persistent migraine headaches that dated back to the time of the wound. They stated I had headaches maybe once a month, while doctor's reports showed every week. EEG tests showed the reading of someone who suffers with seizures. Doctor wrote, "Probably from head wound." He ordered Tylenol.

It didn't make sense for them to avoid all the evidence. I felt my case was a numbers game. Raising any one of my disabilities to the proper rating would have bought me to a one hundred percent rating.

I was not rated fairly for the head wound—only ten percent for headaches. It should have been at least fifty percent by their standards.

Combined, my disabilities gave me a rating of sixty percent. I learned that there was a new law, #4.14, that said if you were rated sixty percent from multiple injuries incurred during one incident you were entitled to an unemployable rating of one hundred percent, assuming the injury kept you from performing your occupation. I figured I had a full compensation rating without any new disability. With a disability rating for PTSD, they had no right, by law, to deny me.

If they had followed their laws from the beginning, I would have been rated fairly. But the new law C.F.R. #4.16 *Total disability ratings for compensation based on unemployability of the individual* now gave me ammunition. What they sent me in their denials didn't match with what I was finding in my records.

It is up to every veteran to find the proof and present it, and that's what I did. Every morning I would write everything out and match up false statements I'd pick out of all the records I had piled up.

The more I got involved, the more I learned how they screwed me over. In one decision, they quoted law C.F.R. #4.16, but only part of it. They left out the part that said, "same incident."

I couldn't sleep at night, worse than ever. I'd talk with John, who had been in SRU with me.

"Look, maybe you should go in, like Joe said, to calm down. It goes on your record if you go in. If you need a ride I'll drive you. No matter what time," said John.

"I tried to go in once but they wouldn't take me," I said.

"With the letter Joe gave you, they've gotta take you, even

if it's in the middle of the night," said John.

"Yeah, maybe. I'm at the edge man, and these damn headaches are driving me nuts."

On a Sunday night, May 10, 1993, I was suffering badly with pain and a migraine. I told Kathy I could call John to drive me to the hospital.

"Are you sure?" asked Kathy.

"Yeah, don't worry. John will take me."

I didn't want Kathy to leave my daughter home alone and John was ready himself to be admitted. I called him about three o'clock in the morning.

"Yeah man, I'll be right over." A half hour later he pulled up. I walked outside with an overnight bag and the letter from Joe.

"Are you all right?" asked John.

"Man, my head is killing me and I just puked all over."

"Well, we'll be there in a few minutes. I'm seeing if they can take me too. I'm like you, ready to pop."

We pulled into the hospital, parked the car and walked into the emergency room. It was empty in the room except for one guy who was sitting in a chair sleeping. We approached the desk. I went first.

"I'm sick as hell. My head has been hurting since Friday. I need a few days to calm down," I said to the nurse on duty. "Here's a letter from the Vet Center."

The nurse took the letter and told me to have a seat. John walked up. They ordered his records and in minutes they were taking him in. John's record showed problems with anger and PTSD. My records didn't show problems with the anger associated with PTSD, yet. They gave me a hassle. Records showing a head wound didn't mean anything.

I walked into the restroom and vomited. My eyes were blurry, I felt dizzy as I looked into the mirror. My eyes were red and so was my face. Sweat covered my body to the point where it gave me a chill. I was shaking as I walked back out.

A doctor called me to the desk. His face didn't show much concern for me, or my condition. I almost begged for help as the doctor ordered me Tylenol, again.

What's with these assholes? I thought. *Is that all they can do—order goddamn Tylenol?*

Then he ordered me back to see a nurse to take my vital signs. By then it was around four o-clock in the morning and I was getting more upset. My blood pressure was high, and so was my pulse.

"Just lay here for a few minutes," said another nurse. "You'll have to see another doctor."

It was a shrink they had on duty that night that I was waiting on; a first for me. She came in and ordered me into a room to ask me some questions. I went through the whole damn thing again and about the headaches.

I started to get emotional about my treatment. I felt as though I was back in Vietnam. I hurt so badly with the headache that I rambled on and on about the killing, the horror, and how I couldn't sleep. The PTSD was a big part in the way I was felling. I was reaching out for help but no one listened.

While I talked with the doctor someone else was checking the computer. They probably saw I had a claim pending, and part of that claim was for PTSD. They wanted me out—sick or not—to screw me over again. But first I had to see the head doctor on call that night. This one really lit my fuse.

"How can I help you?" the head doctor snipped. She was young woman in her thirties with a nasty attitude that immediately got under my skin. It was almost four-thirty. She ordered me two Tylenol with codeine and something else to calm me down.

"I need to be in to calm down. I'm at the end of my rope," I said.

"Are you going to kill yourself?" she asked. She didn't ask

it with a concerned tone in her voice; it was more of a voice
that thought it was a damn game. Maybe she would have
preferred I blew my brains out before I came in. That would
have made her job easier.

The anger raged deep within me. The juices traveled from
my stomach into my mouth, my head and chest felt tight. I
wanted to lash out at her. I wanted her to pay for all the asshole
doctors who ever screwed with me.

"How the hell do I know?" I screamed back at her.

"You don't have a record of any violence. I think you
should go home."

"I'm sick as hell, dammit! What the hell is the matter with
you? Is this the way you treat a veteran? I saved guys in the
field! Is that what I get?" I screamed.

My voice spoke of 'Nam. I really felt weird about that but
it came out. In my mind I was still there. I remembered all the
times I had been treated poorly. 'Nam damaged me and I
wanted revenge.

"Look, we have beautiful woods out here. Why don't you
go and walk around in them and calm down," said the doctor.

"What! Are you crazy? It's still dark out!" I screamed.
"I'm sick and in pain. Can't I get admitted for tests?"

She ordered me to leave.

I cussed the place out. Bewildered, I walked away. The
doctor tried to make me sign a piece of paper stating she
treated me.

"Are you shitting me? I'm not signing shit! You can keep
your damn paper!" I demanded.

She stood there, just looking as I stormed out. John was
already admitted so I had no ride home. At five o'clock in the
morning I didn't want to phone anyone. I left the building
worse than when I came in, and now I was getting drowsy from
the medication.

I decided to walk. I didn't care. I felt worthless and

unwanted. It was twelve miles home down a busy, dangerous highway. I fell to the ground once before leaving the hospital.

I got back up and turned to the darkened building and shouted, "The hell with you! You no good lousy bastards! Who needs you? I won't go into your damn hospital now for nothing!"

Falling down was a turning point. I felt at my lowest. Down, but I wasn't out. They won the round—hell, they won all the rounds. I knew deep in my heart, I was at war. They were against me and I knew that was wrong. Yeah, they were winning the long, hard, disgusting battle, but they were not going to win the war. With all these thoughts in mind, I crossed the highway and started a long, fast pace home. My pain was unbearable but I didn't care. I wanted to torture myself for letting them treat me like they did. I wanted to be punished for being a jerk for so many years. My temper kept me going. I didn't care if a car hit me; I didn't care about anything. All I wanted to do was fight for my rights and I had to stay alive to do this. My stride never let up. I thought back to basic, with Drill Sergeant Martin pushing and pushing. I remember running back to help Sandy on a forced march. He fell back with his bad feet. I wanted to help, but for this, I was ordered to carry him on my back a couple of miles into the camp. I thought of that day and I walked harder. Tight-lipped, I struggled on.

"Fuck them sons of bitches!" I shouted.

I remembered carrying the ninety millimeter recoilless rifle through the mud and waist high water in the swamps of the Plain of Reeds. I was the FNG. They wanted to see what I was made out of.

"I carried the heavy piece of shit, and then some!" I yelled.

"Oh, you did me right, this time. I'll get you back!" I said thinking of the way I was released early from the hospital in Vietnam with an open wound. How I suffered in pain with headaches and they wouldn't do a damn thing. How doctors in Japan said I would get a medical discharge only to be betrayed by an American doctor at Ford Gordon, Georgia.

"You're fit for duty," he said.

"You stupid, son-of-a-bitch! I already did my duty! In 'Nam! Read the goddamn records!" I shouted as I walked along the dark highway miles from home.

I was even pissed off thinking about when I only had about a week left in the Army at Fort Hood. Because some guy didn't want to go out into the field and play war games, I had to go. The captain needed a RTO. Usually you'd have a couple of weeks to get your stuff together to get processed out. I only had a couple of days. We arrived at this base camp and right away I flashed back to Cambodia. I walked into the CP, the command post tent, and saw a guy lying on a cot with his shirt off. He had shrapnel scars all over his body. He rolled over and I thought I saw a ghost! It was another RTO from my company in 'Nam. He had been wounded the same early morning I was. I couldn't believe it. Then simulated mortars started to come in. I hit the ground and covered my head. I felt like I was being tortured, right to the end.

Talking to myself and the accompanying outbursts of anger made the walk easier. I hurt as I took each step. "The more the hurt the better! The better to fight the bastards!" I screamed. How sad this was that I had to battle those who were there to care for the veteran.

I made it to my neighborhood around daybreak. I got curious looks from people walking out for their newspapers, but I didn't care what anyone thought. I'd lived in the same neighborhood for seventeen years. They knew I was a hard worker, had my own business and a nice family. *What's going on with this guy?* they must have thought. Had they known, would they have believed me, much less cared?

When I got home Kathy was already at work and Michelle

was off to school. I phoned my wife and told her what happened. She was upset that I had walked home.

"What if you would have been hit by a car?" she snapped. She was angry, yet her love for me was real. I felt we were drifting, though, and I had to try to keep it all together.

While I was confused and deeply hurt by my experience that night, I vowed to never give up. Something I must have brought home from Vietnam that kept the fight in me. I felt all my psychological baggage was now out on the table, ready to be sorted out into some kind of order, something meaningful. I had most of the facts I needed for my long-awaited VA hearing.

I remembered my drill sergeant's words, "Expect the worse and everything will be all right."

Chapter Sixteen

IN JANUARY OF 1994 I had another appointment with Dr. Smith. I wasn't getting any relief with the pain in the chest so he ordered some tests to be done.

"I want you to see a gastroenterology specialist. I want an endoscopy done on you," said the concerned doctor.

"What's that?"

"They insert a long thin tube down your throat and take pictures."

Why hadn't the VA offered the test to me? I had been hurting long enough. Maybe it had cost too much. Besides, if they found something it could have been used as evidence against them. The mistrust I had for them was overwhelming.

A week later I had a meeting with the gastroenterology specialist Dr. Lieberman. He seemed to be a busy man who just went right to business.

"So I see by your medical history that you were wounded in Vietnam," he said, scanning Dr. Smith's notes.

I wanted him to know everything but felt he was not going to give me much time to explain everything. The specialists I had seen previously were short and to the point. The hell with the small talk as long as I could get some action.

I explained about the back wound and that some shrapnel was still in me. He studied reports and x-rays as we talked.

"Stand up and take off your shirt," said Dr. Liebermen.

I removed my shirt and he stood behind me.

"A nasty scar. Is that where it hurts?"

"Yes, in that area, but it's worse than ever before, and

when I swallow it hurts."

"I think it's all nerve damage from the shrapnel," said the doctor.

I started to get persistent because I needed an answer and he could provide me with that answer.

"Look, something isn't right. I know how I feel. Can't you do that test with the scope to see what's wrong?"

"Didn't the VA do that?"

"Hell no. They haven't done a thing! Dr. Smith said you could help."

"Okay, we'll set up an endoscopy. You'll have it done in the hospital. Go out to the desk and we'll start the paperwork."

"Thanks, doctor. I have to have an answer for this pain; it's been with me to long." We shook hands and he smiled.

I was grateful I found Dr. Smith, because without him I would not have been able to get in for the test.

I filled out the papers, paid for the visit, and then went home. I was told I'd be phoned with the time and day of the exam. Shortly after arriving home they called and told me it would be on March 10, 1994 at eight o'clock. It was several months away, but at least they were taking action.

Things were going along about the same. Then I received a notice from the VA that they had my hearing set for April 19, 1994 at ten o'clock. And they changed my service rep, again. I didn't want another new rep right before my hearing.

I phoned down to the DAV office to talk to my rep. I found out Barry Conners was a Vietnam vet himself.

"Look, can we meet a few times before this hearing?" I asked.

"We'll have a few minutes right before the hearing," said Barry.

"A few minutes! I need more time than that!" I shouted.

There was a silence on the other end of the phone.

"I'll look over your stuff and have plenty of time, trust me.

It doesn't do a bit of good for you to get all excited."

I could tell Barry was getting upset with me and I really wasn't giving him much of a chance. I calmed down.

"I'm a 'Nam vet too. I've been there," said Barry.

"Okay, sorry. This claim has been going on too long."

"I know, and you're not alone. We're swamped with claims."

"Oh yeah, before my hearing I have to go into the hospital for a test."

"The VA?"

"No, on the outside."

"Good. Maybe we can use the report."

I hung up feeling somewhat confident in Barry. He sounded like he would do the best possible for me. I did feel better after I phoned a few guys from the Vet Center to see if they heard of him.

"Oh yeah, he's good," said Jim.

"Yeah, they're all good until I get them," I said.

"Hang in there. They've gotta do something. It's nuts how they do you," said Jim.

I needed the assistance of a veteran's service officer, but this time I wasn't counting on anyone. This time it was all up to me. I would have to present the case. From now on, the only person I would allow to take charge of my life was me.

With past hearings, I'd sit there and not say much, always thinking the right thing would be done, but it never was.

I discovered there was no way I could predict what the board would do with my case. Their reasoning would always be absurd to me. Something blocked the truth. They knew how to use the laws to their advantage and how to keep veterans from discovering the laws that might benefit them. I trusted no one.

The board would send a "Statement of The Case" with every denied decision. They'd list the disability you were trying to increase and explain why they couldn't allow it.

I never paid these statements much thought, but now I began to study them. I could use their language to defend my claim. "I disagree with the decision because it doesn't go along with VA law C.F.R. #4.16. I want the law used in my case, because I feel this was not used before."

I found a lot of mistakes throughout my case. Once I paid more attention to what they were writing, I better understood what I needed to do.

"We can't allow an increase in headaches to the fifty percent rating. To have this you must have headaches more than once a month," one said.

Well that was a no-brainer. My records showed a history of headaches from the day of wound, and my records downtown showed some doctors noted headaches every week. So I wrote them back.

"I disagree with your decision. I'm asking for an increase on headaches because records show *more than one per month* since my wound. I'm asking for you to apply *C.F.R. 4.2 Interpretation of examination reports* to your decision. It fits the situation."

Then I'd make a copy of the reports and highlight in yellow the important facts. Once you got started, it wasn't that tough. The statement from the board helped me figure out what I was looking for in the files. If they said I had to have headaches more frequently than once a month, then I just needed to find the evidence that proved I had them weekly.

I also found books with some VA laws—laws they shouldn't keep from you. They would send copies of certain laws and why they were used in your case, but sometimes their information would be incomplete. Now of course there are websites like http://www.HadIt.com that provide invaluable resources to veterans seeking adequate compensation for their disabilities.

Months passed and Dan was getting more involved with the Vet Center. He was almost ready for the stress unit. Jim also was getting ready to be admitted.

"Man, we caught some hell in the 4th Division," said Jim. "I can't get it out of my mind. Do you think that stress unit helped you?"

"I don't know, Jim. Everyone is different."

Jim's mannerisms, particularly his jitters, reminded me a lot of my old buddy Redman back in 'Nam.

I wished I knew where old Redman was. When I first got home, he came to Florida to visit me. We went out and got drunk, just like we used to back in the enlisted men's club back in Long Binh.

"Hope we don't catch a mortar round, old buddy," he'd said one night in the EM club in 'Nam one night. He was already half shit-faced.

I grinned. I was just about as plastered.

"I'm so jumpy, Phil. After I got hit they had us pinned down big time."

"I know, Redman. That was terrible. I heard it over my horn," I said.

"We were walking up this damn hill and I was humping the radio. All of a sudden we're hit by a rocket," Redman continued.

"'Incoming!' the captain screamed. We were stuck to this fuckin' hill. I'm crawling trying to dig my ass into the ground. Guys are screaming. We had wounded all over. I had to use the radio while my ass was burning from hot shrapnel!"

Redman hung his head and cried. I tried to comfort him the best I could.

Then, in the still of the dark night, we heard a buzz as a few rounds fly into our bunker. We both hit the floor. Redman grabbed his steel pot and jumped down to the lower level where we had a fifty-caliber machine gun mounted and ready to fire. I got on the radio and called in to report we were taking sniper fire.

"How many rounds?" the voice on the other end of the radio asked.

"Three!" I said.

"Who cares how freckin' many!" yelled Redman adjusting his steel pot.

Even in a situation like that one, Redman could make me laugh.

"We're getting shot at!" I continued.

"Do you see anyone?"

"No."

The whole bunker line went on alert but no other rounds were fired in. It was a hit and run. The shots came from a nearby village not far from the bunker line. A moat, strings of concertina wire, trip flares, and claymore mines were between us and the village, but this still wasn't enough to keep out a trained sapper, someone specially trained in demolition and infiltration.

The next day Redman and I were called in to talk with the company commander.

"So how do you know you were shot at?" he asked.

Redman and I looked at each other.

What kind of REMF question was that? I thought.

Starting to laugh I said, "Sir, I've been shot at before."

"Oh, okay, you can leave now."

We saluted and walked away, trying to hold it together. I laughed because we both knew whose ice cream we had been eating only a few days earlier.

"This place is too damn much," said Redman.

✪ ✪ ✪

THAT EARLY MORNING of March tenth came around fast. I

knew the test would find something wrong. There's no way a person could have as much pain as I had with nothing wrong.

Kathy was nervous and I could tell she worried about me. I was just as nervous, but tried not to show it. I just wanted this damn thing over with.

The drive to the hospital only took ten minutes and before I knew it I was lying on a bed with an IV in my arm. It reminded me of the IV I had in my arm when I was wounded.

No use to get all upset. Just lay there and see what happens, I told myself.

They gave me a shot to relax me. Most people fall asleep, but not me. I became sleepy but could still hear what was going on.

I was feeling no pain as they wheeled me into a small room with the equipment needed to perform the endoscopy. I looked around and saw a TV screen and a long black hose hanging on a hook. "Is that thing going down my throat?" I asked.

The two nurses were talking about something funny when Dr. Lieberman walked in. The laughing stopped and they all became serious about their work. I couldn't complain about that.

"How ya, doing?" Dr. Lieberman asked while he checked the equipment and supplies.

"Okay, I guess." I slowly mumbled my words out, almost in slow motion.

"You won't feel a thing—a little discomfort, that's all."

"No problem, doc."

"We'll have to spray this stuff down your throat a few times. Swallow."

The first spray wasn't bad. The second and third tasted like rotten oranges. Soon I was real relaxed and a long black hose was inserted down me. I gagged when I had to swallow, but then it went down fast. There was no pain, just a little discomfort, as the doctor said. Then the doctor could see inside me on a TV screen.

"Man, oh man..." Dr. Lieberman muttered.

I didn't like the tone in his voice.

"What the hell..." he mumbled.

"What?" I tried to gag out.

"Have you been taking a lot of Motrin or aspirin?"

I gave a nod and my heart started to race a bit. He saw something. I saw him shake his head.

"We have to take a few biopsies. We're almost done. Hang in there. You're doing fine," said the doctor.

Soon I was back in a recovery room waiting for him to come talk to Kathy and me.

"I had to take the biopsy to check for cancer," Dr. Lieberman said. "I don't like what it looked like."

I suddenly became numb. Nothing mattered now. No bullshit about the 'Nam or the VA. My life felt in danger and I could only think of my wife and daughter.

"How long did you say you've been hurting?"

"I don't know. Ten years, maybe more."

"They never offered this test to you?"

"No. Only an upper GI."

"That won't show what I found," he said. "They should have performed an endoscopy."

I nodded in disgust. I had ulcers throughout my whole digestive system and severe inflammation of my stomach, esophagus, and duodenum. I also seemed to have a rare disorder called Barrett's Esophagus. People with this have a higher incidence of getting esophageal cancer.

Because of Barrett's Esophagus, Dr. Lieberman wanted an annual checkup. I never smoked and hardly drank that much. If I had, the condition would probably have been worse. The doctor blamed my condition partially from the use of NSAIDs, non-steroidal anti-inflammatory drugs, like Motrin and aspirin.

Years of taking these drugs had done damage to me. He prepared a report that explained my condition so I could use it for my VA hearing.

"I'll call you in a few days with the results," said the doctor.

"Okay, thanks for doing the test."

"No problem. I'm sorry. At first I never would have thought..."

"Yes, the pain is real, and has been for a lot of years. Too bad something wasn't done a long time ago."

"Yes, you're right." He smiled and patted my stomach as a gesture of kindness. He respected what I had been dealing with for so long and he knew it was unfair.

So for about four days I sat on pins and needles fearing I had cancer. I also had to get back in to see Dr. Smith. He had anticipated the ulcers, but the test results proved much more serious than expected. I was ordered on strong ulcer medicine right away.

I was also relieved to find out I didn't have cancer. I was glad I caught it in time. I'd be on medicine the rest of my life and would always have to watch what I ate. Most importantly, each year the endoscopy had to be preformed to check for cancer.

Stress also played a big role in my condition. I knew I had to learn to control my emotions. That was hard to do when Vietnam was always on my mind. The way the VA treated me only made it worse.

I made an appointment with Joe as soon as I had my results. He was disgusted and overly-concerned for my wellbeing. He wasn't acting like the normal VA employee, but rather as another Vietnam vet.

"I'm shot to shit and only get sixty percent. This guy, maybe never in the bush or fired a shot, knows how to whine and bitch and gets a one hundred percent. It's not fucking fair!"

I yelled to Joe.

Joe nodded. "Calm down. You'll have it straightened out soon, I'm sure. I just can't figure it out," he said as he shook his head. "But this new evidence should help."

"You bet your ass it will. They'll hear me if it's the last thing I ever say," I said.

I was now ready for a full-scale war and Joe knew it. He also gave me the feeling he was truly worried about what I might do if I didn't win my case.

"The Moving Wall will be here again. I want you to go."

"Can't deal with it right now, Joe."

"It will be a few days after your hearing. Maybe you'll be calmed down by then."

"Yeah, okay. We'll see."

Joe would take as many vets to The Wall as possible and he'd even made a few trips to The Wall in Washington. "Next time I go to Washington DC, I want you to go," he said.

I couldn't think that far ahead. I had to focus on my upcoming hearing. Now with my new diagnosis and the other supporting materials I had uncovered, I felt was ready for the hearing.

The night before I wrote a four-page statement. I didn't want to blow this. I knew it would all be on tape, so it would be better just to read my thoughts to be recorded—not as I did in the past, ranting like a jerk with a thumb up his ass.

The night before the hearing was rough. I was wired. Do or die. A mission that had to be won. I was going to be the one, this time, doing the shitting on someone else. I was tired of being the one that always got the raw deal. No, this time I had to take control. I could no longer stand by and watch myself and my family go down the tubes while these people screwed my life over. They were wrong and I was out to prove it.

Chapter Seventeen

AFTER WAITING ALMOST two years, my hearing finally arrived. The hearing was my last-ditch effort to present my case and to make someone listen. This time my wife was going to be with me. I needed every bit of evidence possible and she would be the perfect witness.

The hearing was set for ten o'clock in the morning. We wanted to get there early to speak with Barry, my representative from the Disabled American Veterans office. He had prepared an opening statement explaining the issues but I wasn't sure he understood all the facts. I prepared my own statement. This time I armed myself with all the copies of medical records and reports that I'd been gathering for months.

We walked in to meet Barry. When he stood up to greet us I could tell he had lost a leg. It hit me hard.

I'd always felt for those who lost a body part because of the damn war. To me it should have been an automatic one hundred percent rating, but of course it didn't work that way. Losing a leg below the knee was less percentage rating than an inch above the knee. I'd heard guys say. "They should have taken another couple of inches. What the hell difference would it have made?"

I felt as if I was going into battle that morning. It was no wonder. I had no sleep and of course the infamous migraine headache was torturing me again. I knew the hearing would be the most important one I'd ever had. I knew it was truly my last chance; I wouldn't have the will to go on fighting if I lost.

That worried me. I was determined that whatever the

outcome they were going to hear me out and see my anger at the mistreatment of me and my family.

Joe knew the hearing would be a very emotional ordeal for me so he wanted me to stop to see him at the Vet Center afterwards. The Vet Center was only a few blocks away.

We sat at Barry's desk amid a cavernous room with other reps working. Each had his or her own desk and they were partitioned off with half high walls for privacy. After some brief small-talk, Barry opened up with, "Well, we have a slight problem."

"Here we go," I said, my guard going up.

"Well, it's not that bad," said Barry.

"What?" I asked, glancing over to my wife who was already upset.

"They want to disallow the rating you have for the head wound with headaches."

"What are you talking about?" I shouted. "No way! I was wounded to the head and that is it!" I jumped to my feet. My voice echoed throughout the office.

Barry slid back in his chair and didn't say anything. He nervously started to thumb through my folder.

"Let's just go," Kathy said. "The heck with it. We're not begging."

"Hell no! I'm not leaving!" I shouted.

"Look, sit down so we can go over this," Barry said.

"I know what the hell they want to do here. They know I should get more for the head wound and if they take it off they'll boost the PTSD. I'll still get screwed! No way!" I shouted. I was geared up to enter the hearing room. I was ready with all my cannons ready to fire.

"They gave you a low rating for PTSD. I can't understand after studying your record. It should have been more, but we can go on that."

"Mr. Conners, this is why I wanted more time to meet with

you. This is how it is. I got my ass shot up. They didn't care. Now I'm getting what I deserve, what I *need*, to support my family. It's not their fault because my sorry ass got drafted and went to Vietnam, but it was somebody's! That's it, dammit. Get me in there now!" I demanded. My face was on fire and my heart was racing faster than ever. I was probably ready to stroke out.

Barry was at a loss for words.

I paced the office like an animal waiting for the hunt. Kathy was very upset. It hurt so bad to have her witness her husband begging for justice.

"No damn way!" I repeated. "I know what they're trying to do."

"I'll call down to see if they're ready for us," Barry said.

"Good. You get me in there. I'm ready for them."

I refused to let my anger recede. It was pay back time. The nice guy bullshit was all over. They hit a brick wall with me. Hearing panels in the past ridiculed and belittled me, but this would not be the same. There was no panel. It was one-on-one with a hearing officer.

I had studied my case for almost two years. I had enough hard evidence for the board to hand me a rating of fifty percent or more just for the headaches. Adding that to any other single rating and my total would be sixty percent, enough for law #4.16 to kick in.

"So we won't drop the headaches?" asked Barry.

I shook my head no. My eyes were just about to pop out of my head and my migraine was now unbearable. What logic it would be to drop a service-connected combat wound to the head? I just couldn't figure that out. The evidence and scars were there to prove the wound. They couldn't take those away.

"Look," Barry continued, "I have enough here with PTSD alone. They're clearly in error with the low ten percent they gave you for PTSD."

"No, my mind is made up. I was wounded to the head and other areas of my now-hurting body. I want to be treated right and fairly or they can keep everything and shove it up their greedy asses."

"Okay then," Barry said.

I couldn't figure out why he just wanted to key on the PTSD and not for my wounds. Guess the PTSD diagnosis had more weight to it than getting shot up. It was confusing to me, but then I remembered, always think in reverse.

My wife sat there in tears and agreed with me. She still wanted to leave because I was so out of control. She feared they'd lock me up. After all, I was in a federal building. We also had our pride; if it got down to begging for it all, we would have left.

We sat for a moment and I calmed down, but it was easy to see I was a changed person. I was a person I didn't like. I didn't care about that either. As a matter of fact, I didn't care about anything. They made me that way.

Only days before the hearing I had received another "Statement of The Case." It explained how I was going to be denied on all eight issues, even before the hearing. I might go down hard, but I was going to go down swinging.

"Okay, we can enter in about ten minutes," said Barry.

"It's about time. I'm getting sick. My head is pounding badly. Oh yeah, I have something new."

"What?" asked Barry.

I pulled out the doctor's report showing my stomach and esophagus problems. He almost dropped from his chair. I had been so upset that I almost forgot to turn it in to him.

"This is from outside doctors?" he asked.

"You bet. You see why I'm so mad?"

Kathy grabbed my hand hopefully as Barry read the report.

"You have some very crucial evidence that just might turn this thing around."

Barry seemed to take on an even more serious concern. He started to write things down. I could tell he wanted to win this for me. You have to get mad at times to get the point across, but you have to keep the facts straight. I just couldn't walk in talking a bunch of nonsense. If I was going to yell, I'd better be able to back it up.

As we walked down the hall to the hearing room Barry said, "Oh yeah, we have a different hearing officer than they had for you."

"Is that good?"

"Yeah, I think it might be. This guy is fair."

"I hope so," I said.

Barry smiled and we both understood each other better. He was a wounded 'Nam vet. When the smoke cleared, we were as brothers in war.

We entered a small room where a lady was sitting ready to type the hearing, word for word, just like in a courtroom. The hearing officer walked in and introduced himself with a handshake. We took our seats and I was directly across from him, two feet apart, eye-to-eye. In the past I had been sitting way out in no man's land with a panel of doctors asking me questions as if I was on trial.

Barry sat at the end of the table. The officer opened and gave the time and day and mentioned that a tape recorder would be on.

"If your wife wants to stay, she is not to talk unless asked to," he said.

"She's been with me almost twenty-five years and she's not leaving now," I said.

He nodded. "I can make a decision after all the evidence is in and reviewed by the board. If a decision cannot be reached, then your case will be sent to Washington."

I nodded, but I was against sending my case to Washington because it would sit up there for years before a decision would be made. There was a big backlog on cases and it was getting worse by the day.

"I have enough here to prove my case without having it sent to Washington," I said.

Barry opened and for the first time I realized he was well-prepared for my case. He mentioned all the issues that would be covered and, to my surprise, added the esophagus and stomach situation as a service connection due to the overuse of drugs by the VA. I didn't even think of that.

"Also, sir," he continued, "we have records here that show headaches since time of wound and are far worse than noted in the statement of the case."

Barry pulled out doctor reports and the abnormal EEG tests.

"We ask the board for at least a fifty percent rating for headaches, plus for the shrapnel that still remains in his head. He also has been seen at the audio department for over a year now for the tinnitus in his ears. The back wound should be granted more than the twenty percent rating it currently has. It has retained foreign bodies and intercostal neuralgia that keeps him from working."

Barry Conners covered all the issues and then made it a special point to show how the rating board had neglected me with their low rating with the PTSD.

"It is clear in this area he is truly underrated. He should be closer to the seventy percent rating for the PTSD alone."

I was floored on that one but it was true. It was clear for anyone to see how emotionally upset I became when asked to talk about those I lost and about when I was wounded. It was also very easy to see what a short fuse I had, and that was most important. It would be their asses if I went off because I was so angered over some damn wrong decision.

The hearing officer went to work, taking his own notes. He asked me questions and I was straightforward. I even mentioned how I walked home from the hospital in the early morning of May tenth and showed the report. He was very concerned over what had happened and he looked disgusted about it. I felt I was getting through.

Kathy answered questions but was very nervous. "I would have made him go to Canada if we knew this was going to happen." She cried and I took her hand.

"Do you want to say anything?" the hearing officer finally asked.

"Yes, sir. I wrote it down so I wouldn't forget anything."

"That will be fine. Please go ahead and read it."

I took a deep breath and started to speak. I spoke clear and at times had to control myself because I was getting too loud. I didn't want to direct my anger to the officer, but rather to the system.

"I didn't think I'd need a hearing. Over the last few years I've continued to turn in medical reports. Now I'm glad there's a hearing, mainly because I'm more convinced now than ever that the rating board truly does not understand the nature of my wounds." I felt the anger welling up in me again. I paused and took another deep breath.

"The blame is not all the board's, because they only read what doctors wrote—doctors who completely mistreated my condition and wrote down untrue statements and hardly ever reported what I was telling them. This is another issue, and grounds for malpractice that I'll deal with later, after my hearing."

I looked up at the hearing officer and our eyes met. He knew I was as serious as a heart attack. I was in charge, taking control, not like before. I went on with my statement.

"As of now, I want you to understand this back wound. The 'Statement of The Case' explains in the decision about 'Old Shoulder Wound' that entered at the T-6 level. True, but you have to realize the mortar blast landed almost right on top of me. There was a hole about three inches square under my left scapula. At a minimum, this involved the muscle and lung. "When they operated on me they could only remove a large piece of shrapnel. Fragments traveled through out my left chest wall and rib area. Now, common sense will tell you that with an entry wound in the back and fragments in this area, the lungs were involved and nerve damage was done. Abduction of my left arm was noted on the actual date of the wound report." I pulled out the report dated May 26, 1970. I handed it over and started talking again. I had my notes and facts together better than I thought. All those shithouse lawyers in SRU would have been proud of me.

"The right shoulder took a piece of shrapnel from the outside. All the rest entered from the back wound. My head wounds were all the result of the same mortar. All my wounds, the total of sixty percent, are from one incident. They are 'Multiple injuries incurred in action.' This affected many parts of my body system. There's a part in your VA rating law C.F.R. #4.16 for unemployability rating purposes. I'd like this to be used in my case. It fits the situation with my sixty percent rating, a rating that has nothing to do with my PTSD rating. I had sixty percent for wounds without PTSD. I want that clear!"

This was a point that had to be understood and it was important for the VA rating board to know. I knew the law and it was not being used in my case. I was playing their game, holding the cards now. And the new diagnosis with the stomach, which I sure the hell didn't want, was my ace in the hole.

I stopped again. For some reason Barry was trying to talk me out of saying the part about the law or one incident. He thought it might screw me over with the way they did their math. But I was convinced I had a one hundred percent rating coming to me because of wounds only, and now a possible one hundred percent rating alone for PTSD. I wanted all bases covered.

I looked at the hearing officer and he nodded and raised his eyebrows. It was clear to him that I had done my homework and I was not a "Johnny come lately." I've been here before.

"I understand the VA does not pay disability for pain. My shoulder is rated because of loss of range of motion. I want to stress the wound in back makes it hard to lift, push, or pull and years of built-up scar tissue is painful. The intercostal nerve that runs from the spine to or around the rib cage is involved. In addition, arthritis has developed in the areas of all my wounds—traumatic arthritis. VA doctors confirm this as well as the doctors on the outside." I stopped again to take another breath.

"Dr. Smith, the doctor who I'm seeing now because of neglect from VA doctors, has uncovered additional serious health problems. They are life-threatening and were not discovered by the VA because they would not listen to me and my continued complaints!"

There I was, getting louder again. I looked at Barry and he gave me a sign to calm down. My wife took my hand. I looked at her then let her hand go. I was at war and couldn't let up now. I was in too deep.

"The main problem being the source of pain in and around wound area. Most doctors in the past not wanting to do tests probably because they felt I was seeking more disability and wanting to strengthen my case. I feel like they only cared about me getting too much evidence. Their not caring has led to a more serious condition that involves my whole digestive system and esophagus. This is explained from reports from two doctors on the outside and an endoscopy done on March 10, 1994. This shows severe problems, partially the result from the overuse of Motrin prescribed by the VA. This, even after trying and trying for years and years to explain something was wrong. When I eat it hurts! The burning in my chest. Over and over I

begged for tests! In 1992 an upper GI was performed—
nothing. This test won't show this problem. They should have
done a follow-up. I have Barrett's Esophagus that has to be
checked yearly now for cancer!" I screamed, losing control
again. I knew I'd better control myself or I'd blow the hearing.
I took another deep breath.

"My cells in the esophagus are precancerous. This is the
way I understood it from what I gathered from the doctor."

The hearing officer stared at me with a deep concern. I
was getting through. I was mad over the fact the condition
could have been avoided. It was no wonder I was getting upset.
I felt the hearing officer was upset also. I didn't look like a
bum who hasn't done anything for the last twenty years. I was
a guy who was again troubled, because I served a fucked up
year in Vietnam and it wasn't my fault I was wounded.

The VA was formed to help veterans, and the government
had the funds to do this, so why the hell weren't these people
doing what is right? If the system wasn't there it would be
different, but that's not the way it works. We do have a system.
I had been used and was taken advantage of and it was going to
stop. All the mistreatment I went through was finally coming to
a head. Yeah, twenty years later the bullshit had hit the fan. I
continued to speak.

"I'm enraged that the VA didn't find out about my
condition years earlier. If they had, things would have been
better for me health-wise. Now I'll be on stomach medicine for
the rest of my life. This condition should have been found by
the VA. Can you tell me why it wasn't?" I asked the questions;
I was in control.

"This back wound goes a lot deeper than the twenty
percent rating it was given. I also believe this wound was deep
enough to involve the esophagus."

My representative and the officer looked at each other.

"Or, the scar tissue is playing a role in the pain or nerve

damage."

I went on again, explaining severe erosive esophagi was proved by the endoscopy and also prostrate problems that were just brushed aside because of my age. I also mentioned about the swelling that went untreated when I was send to Japan. I popped out a Camp Zama report that proved I was treated for the condition while in the service.

"If you were sick, would you like this kind of medical treatment?" I asked.

The hearing officer just looked at me with disgust all over his face. I felt I had gotten my point across.

The hearing ran over its allotted time, and toward the end the hearing officer asked me questions on PTSD.

"Look," I said, "if you give a rating for PTSD, then you better just look at my record. Believe me, I saw enough over there."

That's all I could say on PTSD without getting mad. He also had the reports from SRU and from the Vet Center. I also turned in a sealed report from Joe.

I was exhausted and emotionally drained from the hearing. I was proud because I could finally walk away from the hearing and hold my head up high. If I didn't get a thing, the hell with it—then I knew in my mind the system was no good and unfair.

I didn't want to believe that, though. I wanted to believe the right thing would be done. I wanted to believe that all these years were just paper mix-ups and my stuff just got into the wrong hands. There's a lot I wanted to believe, but it was hard to believe when you're repeated faced with lies and deceptions.

As we got ready to leave the hearing officer shook my hand again. We looked each other in the eyes. I wanted to make a lasting impression. Eye contact does that.

When the hearing was over, Barry was confident I would do all right. That made me feel better. Kathy and I shook

Barry's hand and left.

"I've gotta see Joe on the way home," I said.

"Okay, it's not far. I'll drive," Kathy said.

My migraine didn't let me argue.

With the hearing over, I could now deal with The Moving Wall again. This time part of my anger should have eased. I now knew some of the reasons for pain. It wasn't all in my head. I was right, and others believed me. Dealing with my emotions might be easier. It would be a time to learn and a time to heal some deep emotional scars. There was time for that now. The hearing was over. All I could do was wait.

Chapter Eighteen

WHEN WE ARRIVED at the Vet Center Joe took us right in.

"Hi, you must be Kathy?" Joe said, offering her his hand.

"Yes, glad to meet you. That hearing upset me," Kathy said.

"Have a seat and tell me. Phil, how'd it go?"

"All right, I guess."

"Yeah, all right until you started to lose it," said Kathy.

"I was ticked when they wanted me to drop the headaches. There was no way I'd do that."

I explained to Joe how I read my thoughts and Joe agreed that was a good way to do it.

"I wanted to leave at first," Kathy said.

"Why?" asked Joe.

"Because of them wanting to disallow his disability rating for headaches when he gets them all the time. They don't have to live with this guy when he's suffering with them."

Joe shook his head and looked at me.

"Look, let's see what's going to happen and maybe you'll calm down some."

I agreed with Joe. I also expressed the concern I had about my stomach and how if I didn't learn how to control myself it would just get worse.

"The Moving Wall is in Brandon. I'm taking the van and I'd like for you to go," Joe said.

"Okay. It's been a while since I last went in 1988. That was emotional."

Kathy nodded.

"Good. We'll leave here around four o'clock Thursday. See you then." We all shook hands and Kathy and I left.

By the time we made it home I was starting to feel better. The day was coming to a close. I had waited a long time for the hearing and was glad it was finally over—I hoped over for good.

Sandy called from Tennessee that night to see how everything went.

"Why don't you come up for a few days? You could use a break," he suggested.

"Not a bad idea, but I hate to drive that far, and the money situation isn't good. I haven't worked for now almost two years," I said.

"Stay with me Phil. It won't cost you anything except gas."

"I'll see. Give me a few days to think about it."

I did feel like getting away for a while. My wife also needed a break, but she had to work and my daughter was still in school. I gave it serious thought, but first I had to handle The Wall again.

I phoned Dan, who had never wanted to go to The Wall. "You want to go?" I asked.

"No, maybe another time," said Dan.

I didn't push the issue. In time he would go. He was talking about attending the stress recovery unit and dealing with The Wall might add stress—stress that he didn't want.

Jim was also about to enter the SRU program but he did decide to go to The Wall.

We arrived at the Vet Center shortly before four o'clock. It was a hot afternoon so I made sure I wore a hat. It said, "We were winning when I left," just like the one I saw the guy wear when I first went into SRU. I put my Purple Heart ribbon on it, along with a 9th Division pin. We used to call our 9th Division patch, "Flower Power" because it resembled a flower of blue and red with a white dot in the middle.

"You all ready?" asked Joe proudly sporting his cap that showed he had been a Marine captain.

We headed down the wooden ramp and the eight of us loaded into a government-issued VA van. The ride took about an hour and it was full of joking around and laughter. It was a way to conceal our emotions. We were all nervous about going to The Wall. You never know how it will affect you. I was still drained from the hearing and now felt vulnerable. My feelings might easily have shown, even without walking up to The Wall.

As we entered the park I could see The Wall. We all became silent. The jokes had already stopped a few miles back. Each man in his own world, doing the thousand-yard stare. The van stopped and we piled out slowly. When I jumped out I had the memory of jumping out of a chopper. Another sick thought. It ticked me off when something would trigger a Vietnam memory.

Men started to separate. I watched as some just drifted away to be alone, not wanting to face The Wall. Too many memories—some good, most bad.

Who the hell wants to deal with this? I thought.

Jim and I walked together. His voice cracked. "Look at all the names."

I gave a nod, not really looking yet.

Joe walked over to us.

"How you two doin'?" he asked.

"Don't know yet," I said.

"Take your time. When you want, I can walk up with you."

"Thanks," I replied with a smile.

"What's that tent for, Joe?" I pointed over to a tent with computers.

"You can look up names. And there's a board over there

that has the names of people looking for people that might have served with a loved one."

"Yeah?" I said.

I walked over to the bulletin board that listed the divisions that served in 'Nam. Under the division name was a list of names of those who died. If you found someone you knew, they'd look in the computer and see who was looking for someone. I searched under my division.

Suddenly my eyes stopped dead, my heart pounded, and the air fell still, just like when I had been pinned down by a sniper. A name, and a bad memory. Robert Washington. Uncontrollably, tears came to my eyes. I thought back to the way we joked only a few days before the nightmare.

✪ ✪ ✪

WASHINGTON AND I HAD been on patrol when we found a large piece of pottery. It was under a lean-to made of bamboo and grass. Most of us hadn't used a real toilet in months. The perfectly-shaped clay pot was a welcome sight. You take a lot for granted in life. Using a real toilet at that time in my life was one of them.

"Man, a nice place to take a break," I said. "Anyone have a toilet paper?"

"Sure do," said Three-Six, "but rank has its privileges. Get in line."

We all took turns sitting on this orange clay pot with a comfy rim. It was a lot better than sitting over a log. Washington was laughing. I remembered that. It was one of the first times I ever saw him laugh. He was new to our platoon, but not new to Vietnam.

Why had he come back?

I shook my head.

✪ ✪ ✪

"FIND SOMEONE?" JOE asked, noticing my reactions.

"Yeah, Washington."

"Okay, let's see who's looking for someone who knew him," said Joe.

We walked over to the tent and I tensed up.

"Can I help you?" asked a nice lady working for the In Touch Program. I handed over the name I wrote down. She quickly brought up an entry on the computer.

"It's his daughter, Cheryl. She's looking for someone who knew her dad."

I thought I was going to faint. Joe grabbed my arm to steady me. Jim stood there silent and in a daze.

When I heard it was his daughter, I could only think of my own daughter Michelle and how lucky I was to have her. I was grief-stricken to think this girl's dad died in Vietnam. The fact that I was the last person to ever talk to her dad made me feel close to her. I had the need to reach out to her, to comfort her and tell her he was at peace now.

"Are you going to write her?" Jim asked.

"I want to. I want to tell her he didn't suffer and that he loved her. He had a wife and four kids. I remember him telling me that," I said.

Guilt overcame me. I didn't have any kids back then, while he had four. Was it right that I lived instead of him?

There wasn't any correct answer to a question like that. I have a daughter and that was meant to be. I accepted that, but I couldn't accept the absurdity of this man dying when he had so much to live for.

We loaded back into the van just before sundown. I didn't talk much, just thinking about what to write Washington's daughter. Her name was Cheryl and she lived in New York. I remembered Washington telling me about his family when we talked on his last night.

When I got home that night I couldn't sleep so I wrote the letter. I told her I was with her dad when he died and he was a hero. He didn't suffer and never knew what hit him. He was asleep when we took the mortar round. I told her he loved her. I told her to write if she'd like and I'd tell her anything I could about her dad. The letter was short and to the point. The main thing I wanted to get across was that he didn't suffer and he died believing he was doing the right thing. He served his country with honor. He was brave and proud to be in the Army. I also was proud of him.

I mailed the letter the next day, hoping she was still at the same address since the request was almost a year old.

That morning while I was alone, I also wrote the local newspaper. Washington's memory deserved much more and I wanted others to remember those who died in Vietnam. This is what appeared in the St. Petersburg Times on Monday, May 30, 1994.

Veteran Can't Erase a Vietnam Memory
by Phil Ferrazano

My visit to the Vietnam Memorial Moving Wall in 1988 when it came to St. Petersburg was a very emotional and moving experience. It uncovered many buried thoughts about a place and time I'd like to forget but can't. Being a wounded vet makes it all the more difficult to forget, and a continuing struggle with the VA has made me bitter and angry, so I won't allow myself to forget.

I was invited to go on a trip to The Wall again last week while it was in Brandon. At first I didn't want to go, thinking, why stir up emotions again? I decided to go anyway. To my surprise, it was more emotional than my first visit.

When we arrived we walked over to a tent with a computer and a bulletin board with a list of names. They were names of people who died in Vietnam and their loved ones wanted to find people who knew them over there. As I searched under the 9th Division, I came upon the name of a man who was killed next to me May 26, 1970. We were on a mission in Cambodia. He and others were killed when we came under a ground attack by the North Vietnamese Army. We changed places shortly before the mortars came in and we took the first hit. I believe he never knew what hit him. It left me with wounds and the lifelong question, why him, not me?

For twenty years, I've lived with this memory always on my mind. I always felt maybe I should contact one of his family members to tell them he did not suffer. Maybe it would help them and me. But I didn't know how until now. I have given thanks to the In Touch Program, set up by caring people who were working at The Wall.

I was able to get an address and phone number of a family member. I broke down when I found out it was his daughter who had posted the inquiry about her father's friends. I thought of my daughter and of him talking to me that night before he died. He told me about his four small kids and his family. He also told me about why he made the choice to make the Army a career and come back to 'Nam for a second tour. That tour was only into its third week when he died. He was only twenty-one years old.

I guess his daughter and family always wondered how he died and whether he suffered. So I wrote her the next morning. I'm waiting for her reply. I was the last person to ever talk to him. I told her he was a hero earlier that day and he died believing he was doing the right thing.

Memorial Day always has been a sad time for me, with its memories of my wounds and the deaths of others I knew. This one might be less painful, since it gave me the chance to get rid of something I've been carrying around for twenty-four years. I hope it makes his family feel better too.

I have to thank the good people who work at The Wall, who handle this In Touch Program and Joe Adcock, who is team leader at the St. Petersburg Vet Center. He is a Vietnam veteran who has made a lifelong commitment to help fellow vets.

Let's not forget the true meaning of Memorial Day.

That article touched many people that Memorial Day. I was happy it had appeared when it had. I had been wounded on Memorial Day weekend and it was a particularly difficult time of year for me.

Early the morning the article appeared in the paper I got a phone call. "Hi, are you Phil?"

"Yes, I am."

"I just read your article. I wasn't in Vietnam but I'm a World War II vet. I just want to say thanks. That article touched me. Welcome home."

I didn't know what to say. I had a lump in my throat.

"Thanks," I managed.

Soon, another call.

"I'm a 'Nam vet. Thanks brother. Welcome home. God bless you."

The calls continued throughout the day. Even weeks later I'd get a call now and then.

I'm glad I wrote the article. It helped not only me, but also other vets who had memories to deal with. I thought expressing my feelings would help others. I was right, it did. Memorial Day that year was a little easier to bear. I was proud to have served, which was a feeling I needed. To finally have that feeling was as if I overcame a major hurdle.

That Memorial Day night, after almost twenty-five years, I opened my old duffle bag and pulled out a small black case that protected my Purple Heart Medal. I displayed it on a shelf in my home office.

Kathy walked in as I was putting it on the shelf. "What's that?" she asked.

"My Purple Heart," I said, ready to cry.

"I love you," she said.

"I love you too, honey. Sorry it's been so tough on us."

"It's been tougher. We'll be okay."

"I'll try to change."

"Why? Some things are better left alone," she said with tears in her eyes.

I could only smile with the lump that came to my throat. We hugged and kissed. I wanted her to know that I wouldn't let her down. She also knew I'd fight for us till it was over, no matter what happened. The ordeal we faced seemed to bring us closer together. If we lost it all and were down to nothing, one thing was for sure, we would always have each other.

Chapter Nineteen

I HAD JUST MADE a cup of tea in my quiet kitchen. Kathy was off to work, and Michelle at school. The bag was still steeping as I walked to the mailbox. I grabbed the mail and noticed a thick envelope from the VA Regional Office. I knew it was the decision. I couldn't believe how fast I got it. It had only been a couple of weeks. I couldn't open it. I set it on the table with my heart pounding.

"A letter! A God damn letter. I can't believe I'm afraid to open it!" I said while I took the bag out of the cup. I took a sip as I walked over to the table and sat down. "Let's just face the music again; let's see how they're gonna screw me over," I said. I was getting mad and hadn't even opened the damn letter yet.

Did I do enough to get my point across to those who made the decisions? Would they ever give me what I deserve? Would the biggest fight of my life be over? Would I get the decision I needed to continue with my life and for my family? After all these years it was down to this.

"Go ahead, open it," I said to the empty kitchen. "What can they do, send me back to Vietnam?"

With a deep breath, I opened the letter. I glanced over the first page and thought maybe it was someone else's. Everything was in my favor. All issues were covered and a new percentage rating had been assigned to each of the existing disabilities. The headaches alone had been raised to the fifty percent level. After I read that I knew I'd be at the one hundred percent. And I was! The board determined from all evidence that I was now a one hundred percent disabled veteran for the wounds I received in Vietnam.

My stomach and esophagus conditions were service connected because of all the medication I took over the years. My right shoulder was finally recognized and rated. The only issue not rated was the edema that I suffered with and was sent to Japan for treatment. They still felt the swelling was a childhood-related medical condition. That still upset me but I was covered with the one hundred percent and all my medical needs would be taken care of now. How did I feel?

I cried. I was simultaneously sad and happy. Sad, because this all had to happen and my health was not like I wanted it to be. Happy, because they respected me and did what was right. It could have been determined years ago if someone had done their job. They were in clearly in error, and I do feel I had the right to continue with a malpractice claim, but when Barry phoned me with more news, I decided not to.

"They did you one better," said Barry.

"What?" I asked.

"You're permanent and total."

"What does that mean?"

"They can't mess with you. No future exams to try and cut you out. And there are additional benefits like funding for your daughter's college, license plates, and base exchange privileges. The whole ball of wax."

I was speechless.

"Thanks, Barry. You did a good job for me."

"That's all right," he said. I'm sure he was smiling on the other end of the phone.

I now had a new title. Could I adjust? A major battle had been won and my coping skills work a little better. However, I was still angry but had no one to direct the anger towards. For years it was always directed to the VA and I couldn't do that now. The pain was still there along with the headaches, but now I was getting proper medication and I was trying not to get mad or pissed so easily. Old habits are hard to break and my temper would still get the best of me when I let it. At times I felt like a caged animal just wanting to bust loose.

I became more of the loner, avoiding everything that might bring on stress. My stomach and ulcers deserved a rest. I had just relived Vietnam again through my memories and through the words of others. I struggled with my journey back in time, a time that seemed to never go away. I was starting to accept some things about war and realized I was part of history. It was in the books now as to how we were used. We were misled into believing we would win and everything would be all right. We were only asked to do a year in Vietnam, a year that affected many for a lifetime.

My Vet Center meetings continued and so did my one-on-one meetings with Joe. There wasn't anyone happier than Joe to hear I was granted the one hundred percent.

"It's about time!" Joe said. "There's no way they could have turned you down this time."

He also stated that by my taking control and finding outside doctors who found some medical answers probably helped. I agreed and I thanked God, I did. I could have died without the proper medication, which the VA now provided. I was actually being treated well.

"If you need a break from these meetings, it's up to you," Joe said.

I knew my problems were not solely the result of a string of previously-denied claims. It was much deeper than that. I didn't feel ready to just walk away from my group sessions with guys I knew and trusted. I had respect for each man knowing they also had struggles. And I wanted to stay on partly to shine some light in their tunnels. Let them learn from me. It's not that I was a damn expert on the VA rating process, but it was the fact I didn't give up. If you believe you are right, then fight. I hoped I could be an example for denied vets everywhere.

Never let up or you'll lose. I would not allow myself to be a loser in their eyes, or in my own heart. My heart had been broken over and over again. At times I felt like it broke beyond repair. Then I remembered a song that said, "A heart must have been broke before it starts to mend."

It was coming together and I was writing everyday. I would keep my doctor's appointments and tried hobbies like oil painting. Once in a while I even started to play my guitar again. The motions were there but the heart wasn't. The only thing that would really interest me was the writing. In my words I could relive my experiences while still searching for that damn lost piece of the puzzle. I hoped the words I wrote would help me heal.

Days after the decision was handed down to me, I got another jolt. It was Mother's Day. My mom, wife, daughter and I were having dinner. The phone started to ring. I jumped up and walked into my home office to answer it.

"Hello," I said.

"Yes, hello. Is this Phil?"

"Yes it is."

"I just got your letter. I moved from New York out here to California. I'm Robert Washington's daughter Cheryl. Did you know my dad?"

My heart jumped into the pit of my gut. My eyes filled with water. I couldn't talk and felt like I was going to break down. After a short pause I spoke. "Yes, I did."

"I'm so excited you wrote me. Can you tell me a little about him? I wasn't even born yet when he died."

I was at a loss for words but needed to say something to this sweet-sounding voice. I only could think of a little girl wanting her daddy. Like my own daughter depended on me, she needed something. She was a grown woman and never knew her dad. It broke my heart.

"He was next to me when he died. He was sleeping and never knew what hit him. He didn't suffer, if that helps."

"A plane crash is what I always heard. That's what I think they told my mother."

Again, I was speechless. He died on the ground next to me in Cambodia.

"No honey, he was on the ground next to me in Cambodia. He was a hero. He died doing what he believed in," I said.

She was as confused as I was over the fact they said he was in a plane crash. Nothing should have surprised me about what was written down. It was a big records screw up as far as I was concerned. I thought of my own records the day I was discharged and how they said everything was lost.

"I'll write you," she said. "Maybe we can meet? My whole family wants to meet you."

"Sure, maybe one day. One thing, though. How many kids did he have?" I asked.

"Four."

"I just wanted to make sure I had it right."

Cheryl, who I was talking to, hadn't been born yet, but he had already counted her as another one of his kids.

"He loved you all a lot. Thanks for the call," I said.

We promised to stay in touch and she thanked me also. We hung up and I never heard from her again. We made contact and she learned something about the dad she never knew. It eased both our minds that day. Maybe that was enough. Maybe we'll still meet one day.

Kathy now knew who I was talking to. We all had tears in our eyes. It was good to say to someone, "Hey, this guy was good, a hero, my friend." In a way I felt he was sent to 'Nam a second time to save me. He had asked to change places with me only moments before the deadly mortar round landed and that changed the lives of so many. One split second and the course of our lives headed into a different path. The paths we take in life are many and our paths were altered because of Vietnam. Was it meant to be that way?

Memorial Day was easier as I thought of Washington and the others. I remembered Williams, Bunny, Orgeron, Crowe, Murphy, Sapp, Lewis and the others I saw on The Wall. Memorial Day had true meaning to me, now more than ever. I knew men on The Wall for whom we have a holiday. As a kid I remembered the old guys wearing hats and saluting the flag at the parades with tears in their eyes. Now I shared those sentiments.

The summer ended like all the rest. And before we knew it another holiday season was around the corner. I wanted to make this one better than the last few had been. All my Christmas holidays as a kid were great—a family time. It didn't matter what was under the tree for me.

I thought of how we were married while I was still in AIT three days before Christmas and how the next Christmas I was in Vietnam. But I was close to the end of my tour and got to see the Bob Hope Show. The show was something to remember. I thought of those in the bush who needed a break from the war and should have been able to be at the show. Somehow it didn't seem fair.

For many vets, the holidays would only bring on bad memories. A happy time often will bring on a hardship. I hated that. I hated the fact that some can only relate to the holidays as a time when a friend got killed or a booby trap took a leg off on Christmas eve, or a position was overrun on Thanksgiving. That's what Jimmy remembers. And John was wounded on Thanksgiving.

"I hate it. Never leave the damn house on that day," John said to me.

"Come over this year for Thanksgiving," I said.

He did, and his wife appreciated it. "It's the first time," she said.

It made my day, and I hoped his. I even played my guitar and sang a little. Still sounded terrible. Some things never changed. I had to work on it.

As winter approached the days were getting shorter. By the time Jim and I walked up to the wooden ramp at the Vet Center it was dark. This night it was even darker. More people were there than usual.

"What's up?" Jim asked me.

"Don't know. What's with all the cars?" I said.

We looked at each other and walked into a room where everyone had strange looks on their faces. Joe walked in looking like he just saw a ghost. "Everyone in?" he asked.

No one was talking. The staff knew what was up and so did a few of the vets. "If you haven't already heard, one of our members killed himself yesterday," said Joe.

"What?" I said.

"Who?" said another.

"Why?" another asked.

We felt sorry for a fellow 'Nam vet who gave up.

"It was Roger," said Joe.

I knew him, but not well. He was a member who had been coming to the Vet Center for years. He had special feelings for veterans and he was always there to help one out. This time no one was there that could help him.

"He was my only true friend. He would take me to the hospital when I needed a ride," said Ron, a vet who had lost a leg in 'Nam.

He couldn't talk anymore. Others spoke of their memories of him.

Why now? He had it together, I thought.

"He started school, got an increase on his VA disability and had a girlfriend," another said.

No one had the answers. He shot himself while on a trip to

a cabin in up state New York where he grew up. Maybe a phone call to his girl friend triggered something? No one could say and I didn't know. Some who were close knew him better and some probably knew why. What was certain though was he did suffer with his memories of the Vietnam War.

I was in a state of shock like all the others. Knowing how depressed I could get scared me. Could I get that low? I feared that maybe I could. Maybe at times suicide would be easier. It would not make it easier for the family you left behind. Why should they be left to deal with your problems? They shouldn't. I drilled that into my head. I couldn't allow myself to become weak.

Jim and I walked alone to our cars.

"What's it all about, man?" he asked.

I just looked at Jim with no answer.

"'Nam vets are killing themselves, and if they don't, Agent Orange will do it," said Jim.

Jim told me of a friend he had who died. It was Agent Orange. Only the year before while he made a trip to The Wall in Washington, he ran into a guy who served with him. They were on Hill 875 together. They were both standing next to each other at The Wall, and then started to talk. They realized they served together and were friends over in Vietnam.

Then a year later Jim got a call. His friend had died. His friend's wife blamed it on his exposure to Agent Orange. Jim went to the funeral and now he had to go to Roger's funeral.

Dan was now in SRU and met Jim in there.

"How's Dan going to do up there?" I asked.

"Don't know—he's a trip. He saw some heavy action," said Jim.

"I know. We went over together. I'm worried about him," I said.

I didn't like this suicide shit. I was once told that more 'Nam vets had committed suicide than are names on The Wall.

Many felt their names should be added. After all, 'Nam did it to them.

My head would hurt when we talked of suicide. It made me think too much. There was talk of it back in the bush, especially as the rain pounded you into a rice paddy at night.

We slept on a paddy dike, cold and wet to the bone with only a foot or so to balance our asses from falling into the water of the paddy. In a ball and covered with a poncho, nothing seem to help. The night never ended and this night seemed the worst. I wanted to give up. I felt worthless.

A friend crawled over. The rain was so hard I couldn't even see his face. I could see a little glitter off his steel pot. "Got a razor blade?" he asked.

"What?"

"I want to kill myself," he said.

I was so depressed I felt it was a good idea. At that second I had the feeling it could be done and it would be easy. Putting the M-16 to your head would have done the trick.

"No man, morning will come. We'll make it. We'll be out of this freckin' swamp soon. Hang in there," I said, trying to convince myself to do the same.

"Yeah, you're right," he cried hanging his head and pulling his poncho over him. Morning came and the torturous rain let up. We were still in 'Nam and we had made it through another night. Now I could relate. Morning will come again. I wasn't in a rice paddy again, only my mind was. I could handle it.

Things were starting to work out for me so I had to keep thinking positive. What the else could I do? Either think positive or wind up like Roger. I refused suicide—if I didn't do it in 'Nam that night, then why now? It didn't make any sense, but 'Nam didn't either. The fight within me continued.

Chapter Twenty

DEALING WITH THE suicide of a fellow Vet Center member was hard. It was new to me, but in some demented way it fit. Everything seemed to tie into my tour of Vietnam in one way or another.

When I had my meetings with Joe I could see how the suicide clearly upset him. Jim was also taking it hard. Dan was in the VA hospital going through the stress recovery program. The holidays were getting closer and I thought it wouldn't be a good idea for Dan to be in the hospital. It wouldn't be easy talking about Vietnam while the Christmas season was upon us.

"You'll be up there during the holidays," I said.

"Fuck the holidays. They didn't give a shit about us during Christmas in 'Nam. Don't mean shit to me now," Dan said with his usual negative attitude.

It hurt me to hear him talk as he did, but that's the way he felt. Every day was the same to him. At least now it was his turn to deal with what he had gone through in Vietnam. I listened as he had to me, even though I worried about how his stress impacted my own still-fragile state.

"Hey, did you know the guy who bought the farm?" he asked.

"A little," I said, not wanting to dwell on the suicide.

"What'd he do, blow his fuckin' brains out?" he asked coldly.

The thought of death didn't seem to bother him. He was numb to it. He saw too much during his tour of duty. He was unfairly subjected to months of horror without a break.

Remembering what he saw and had to do troubled him. This was a big part of his anger.

"Never had a break, man. After the 9th went home I was with the First Cav, humping my sorry ass all over the 'Nam," he said. "Where did you go?"

I told him, like I had a thousand times before. While he was still on the line, I was doing security up in Long Binh. Dan talked in circles, still screwed up on certain events that happened.

"I can't get Cambodia out of my head. How about you?"

"The same here," I said.

We both rattled on with the same old conversation. I listened because he needed it. As Dan talked my mind drifted off. I had the honor of going out with Bunny and another new guy one night while close to the Cambodian border. For some strange reason we were going by the book that night. NVA were in the area and the captain wanted a body count.

I wanted to mind my own damn business.

It was a heavily wooded area, different than the mush of the delta. We headed out; I had the Prick 25, PRC-25, the standard radio we used in 'Nam, strapped to my back like a permanent fixture. Prick was a good nickname for it. It was good thing we had them, though. They saved a lot of people. Also killed a lot, particularly the walking targets who had to carry them. The Viet Cong knew that the radio was the heartbeat of the unit and without it you were almost helpless. Knock it out and the officer next to it, and they accomplished a lot.

It was just about dark as we walked down a trail. I didn't like taking a trail but it was quieter than banging through a pile of brush. I just wanted to find a nice comfortable spot to lay my weary body down. All day we had humped in this new area. At one point during the day we lined up against a hill, spread apart so each man was his own point man.

Signs were posted in Vietnamese saying "Beware Booby Traps." We walked slowly and with every step it seemed like you were closer to getting your shit blown away.

Someone screamed and we all hit the ground. One guy fell into a pit. A pungi stake—a very sharp bamboo stick, usually smeared with human waste so you'd get a nasty infection—took a piece out of the side of his leg.

"Fuck this bullshit, using our asses for this bullshit!" I said with my heart throbbing. The detail was too hazardous. The war was getting more and more absurd. Many wondered if being there was even right.

Talk of a mutiny was a good idea at that moment. Most would take jail over being made to do something you knew could get your ass blown away.

The captain backed us out. I called in a dust-off. It upset everyone when one of us got hurt, especially over orders that we knew were wrong. The gooks were even telling us there were traps everywhere and we still walked in. Our lives at times seemed worthless. To be used as we were was disgraceful.

Later, we learned the guy who fell into the pungi pit lost part of his leg. It was hard to believe because it didn't look that bad. "He's going back to the world?" was our first reaction to the news. Some wished they had fallen in the pit. It didn't take much to get an infection with the dirty conditions over there.

It pissed me off. They had released me from the hospital into that fucking sewer with an open wound. Death by NVA or death by Army doctor—what was the difference?

We settled down into our listening post position, the three of us. I was beat to hell and was still thinking of the pungi pit and how lucky I was not to land in one. The air was cool, almost cold. The nightly rain started. We huddled close to one another and draped our plastic ponchos over our heads.

The only sound was the drizzling rain hitting the brush.

Tap, tap.

Then the rain became a downpour. I called in a situation report trying to keep the radio low. A trained enemy ear could easily hear the crackling sounds the radio would make. That worried me.

As always, it was hard to stay awake. We took turns on guard, but I never slept on LP.

"I hear something," I said.

"What?" asked Bunny.

"Movement."

"What do we do?" he asked like I had the damn right answer. Me, a four-month-in-country, green, PFC.

We crawled closer into the brush away from the trail, which seemed like it led into a few different directions. *Maybe this wasn't such a good spot to lie down*, I thought.

Soon I could hear a large group barreling towards us. I thought I would shit a brick. GIs don't walk fast at night. I knew it must be NVA. I radioed in.

"Any friendlies out here?" I asked.

"No," came the crackling response.

"We have a platoon size, heading our way."

"Okay, sit tight."

"Yeah, no shit. We can't move. We'll just lie here and get ready."

"Roger that."

"Yeah, roger out."

I turned the radio off thinking we were screwed royally this time. I knew we were no damn match against a platoon of NVA.

"Stay down. Don't talk. Let them pass us," I whispered, hoping the darkness would conceal us.

No one made a sound. Our lives were on the line big time if they spotted us, heard us, or if they stopped to take a piss in front of us. I think all three of us already pissed our pants and if their senses were keen enough they would have smelled that. You couldn't take anything for granted with the enemy. The more I learned, the more I respected them.

With each step they made, my heart skipped a beat. I was sure they could hear me breathe. I tried to hold my breath. They walked within ten yards of us. I could see their small frames carrying AK 47s.

I pressed my finger against the trigger of my M-16. I was ready to open up, but we couldn't panic and just open fire. It would have been suicide. If we had been able to see better then it might have been different. But our job was to listen and report in so that's what we did. They passed us and headed toward our platoon and the rest of the company. I only hoped they were ready.

"You guys all right?" I said.

"Can you believe it?" asked Bunny.

"Let's stay down; something is gonna happen."

Then all hell broke loose. The cracks of M-16s were going crazy. Red tracers were coming in our direction.

TA! TA! TA!

The gooks were returning fire as they ran back toward us. Green tracers from the AK 47s were aiming toward the red. *Crack! Crack! Crack!*

Ain't this a pisser, I thought. We had red tracers and they had green. Their weapons had a distinctive sound and so did ours. It was like it was planned that way, the rules of the game. Except none of us wanted to play their damn games.

They passed us again. M-79 rounds were hitting.

Pop, boom!

Claymores were set off. We were caught in crossfire. I put the radio back on. In a flash they were gone, into the night. I thought with the choppers we owned the night; but no, the NVA did. The dead of night is when they moved and we were in their backyard. They marauded through the jungle with the swiftness and certainty of a pack of wolves.

That's something we learned to respect, like the song "Here Comes The Night." With the night you'd better be ready. Don't take anything for granted. They were at war while we just wanted to get our lousy year over and get home before Jody took our girl.

I remembered marching through the chilly hills of Fort Benning, Georgia in basic training. The smell of pine trees and dew filled the air as we sang, "Ain't no use in going home. Jody's got your girl and gone."

I didn't worry about Jody. But some had already lost their girls to this Jody guy. We hated that little chicken shit. Never met a guy named Jody. Guess Johnnie Taylor planned it that way—didn't want us all getting back stateside and beating the hell out of the first poor SOB we met named Jody.

"They're gone! Stop shooting!" I screamed over the horn.

What a long hard day. We fired off thousands of dollars worth of ammo while these bastards were already hiding in the ground somewhere.

✪ ✪ ✪

"THAT WAS A FUCKED up night," said Dan still on the phone.

"My heart still races when I think it."

"Yeah, I hear ya buddy. What a day."

"Look I gotta go. I'll call ya later," I said.

"Sure, take care man."

Restless from our talk, I sat up most of the night. I wondered about some old friends and why I hadn't heard from Chris.

Thanksgiving was only days away when we were alarmed again at the Vet Center. The same situation. Jim and I were walking up to the ramp and I had that weird feeling again.

Something was wrong.

"Who did it this time?" asked Jim.

"Oh man, can't take this anymore," I said.

"Now it's Thanksgiving again. I hate it," said Jim. "That's when we took Hill 875. Thanksgiving Day, noon, 1967. Two companies of the 4th Division and a battalion from the 173rd Airborne met at the top of this fucking hill."

I knew about the battle at Dak To. It was the worst—272 killed including three Medal of Honor winners, all for a piece of shit hill. Jim's whole body shook when he remembered the nightmare.

"Yeah, I guess I have something to be thankful for on Thanksgiving. I made it off that hill when so many others didn't," said Jim. "I was just a PFC. I remember all the sergeants were killed. Reporters where waiting at the bottom of the hill and they quickly stuck a sergeant pin on me because they didn't want the public to think we lost most in charge. Ain't that some shit? Ya ever heard anything like that?" Jim asked.

"Nothing I hear now surprises me, Jim."

Jim felt guilty celebrating Thanksgiving and I could see why. When we entered the center the gloom was all through the place.

"Who did it this time?" I asked.

"Burton," someone said.

I was in shock. He was a guy we all looked up to. We thought he had his life together. He had a good business and nice home. None of that seemed to count. He must have been more troubled by his time in 'Nam than he ever let on. At The Wall I remembered how he just sat on the grass looking at it from a distance. He couldn't walk up. He stayed alone. I never realized how the war affected him until that day. I knew he was hurting but never thought he could kill himself.

Joe was a mess. He had been close to Burton.

Silence came over the room. We all had tears in our eyes. Two suicides, so close together. And yet there were more. Another vet who died earlier that week might also have been a suicide. They didn't know yet. Others started to question if going to the Vet Center was the right thing. Did it bring back too many bad memories?

Hell yes it did. What could you do? Keep the memories bottled up for the rest of your life? Was it healthy to always talk about Vietnam? I really didn't know. I knew finding answers to some of my many unanswered questions helped me. But that was me; everyone is different.

The meeting broke and we all said a prayer and hugged.

I grabbed Joe's hand and gave him a firm shake. I couldn't talk. My eyes told it all. We all left the Vet Center. Another sad drive home. Nothing had changed in the last few years. I was still trapped back in Vietnam.

It was only a few minutes after I walked into the house and the phone was ringing. I picked it up. I already knew it was Dan. Word traveled fast about a vet killing himself.

"How you doing up there, Dan?" I didn't mention the suicide. I thought it would mess with his head.

"Listen to this shit. I walked outside to the dock this morning around seven. Got my coffee and smoke. Then I saw a guy lying there with his fucking brains splattered all over the grass. He shot himself, man. I found him and the gun."

"I knew the guy," I said softly, not wanting to hear anymore.

"No kidding? He knew how to do it. Blood all over the place, tongue hanging out."

"Don't even tell me. I don't want to know."

"Fuck it man, don't mean nothing."

"Oh man, come on. I knew the guy."

"A security guard comes over and almost pukes, asks me, 'Don't this shit bother you?' I looked at him and said, 'Saw the same shit in 'Nam. Fuck it.' The guy gave me a weird look."

"Take it easy, Dan."

"The guy had guts, man. Couldn't deal with this shit any longer," said Dan.

"Don't get any ideas," I said.

Dan laughed.

"That's not guts, cutting out like that. Guts is sticking around. Got it?"

"Yeah."

"Got it?" I repeated.

"Yeah, I got it." His tone was softer. He was hurting over this. It did him no good to be the person to find the body of a fellow Vietnam vet. And why did Burton kill himself on the VA hospital grounds? Had he been reaching out for help?

Burton's job was in demolitions. He said he felt bad that his job killed a lot of people—kids, women, anyone that traveled into the paths of his work. He saw the aftermath of his job and it stayed with him, no doubt till the end, on a lonely dark night.

Days later, after dinner, my phone rang again. I got to where I hated the ring of it. Sometimes I'd actually be afraid to answer it.

What now? I'd say to myself. Usually it was a call for my daughter. That didn't bother me, because that meant if she used the phone I wouldn't have to. This time, though, the call was for me.

"Phil, it's Chris."

"Old buddy!" I said.

It had been over twenty years and I knew the voice right off. We both started to laugh.

"Where the hell are you?"

"Live in Texas, close to Dallas. Bill told me you were trying to get in touch with me."

"Yeah, how you been? What are you doing?"

"Well, I'm married, have two kids and have my own business."

"Great! What do you do?"

"I counsel disabled vets and deal with guys with PTSD."

"What, you have to be kidding me?"

I couldn't believe Chris was working with vets, and then I remembered getting a book from the library titled *Strangers at Home*. Chris had been featured in the book. As a grad student in the early seventies, he had been involved in a study about how Vietnam vets adjusted to life back in the States.

"Was that you involved in that book?" I asked.

"Hell yes. That was tough. I was burned out from working on that study."

"Bill said you got one hundred percent from the VA. You sure the hell deserve it. I remember all the hassles you went through after you were hit," Chris said.

"Yeah, I wanted a letter from you to help my case," I said.

"Now you don't need it, but if you ever do I'll write one. I was there with you. When I heard you got what you deserved, I cried."

I didn't say anything. Chris was sincere and that meant a lot to me.

We hung up and said we'd stay in touch with each other.

I was glad I had found Chris again. I was also glad I found Three-Six and had the chance to talk with Washington's daughter. Things were coming together for me. In my heart I knew things couldn't be like they were in the past, but I wanted to learn to accept the way I was living. I wanted to learn to control my emotions when talking or thinking of Vietnam. A couple of years had passed when I felt a change or a cleansing going on within me. Still, I think of Vietnam daily and I still suffer with pain, though having the proper medication has helped.

It took a sad event to open my eyes one day. It was at a

funeral. I hated going to funerals so I always tried to avoid them. This one I couldn't. The friend was too close and dear to me and many others.

Chapter Twenty-One

I WAS SITTING AT the table sipping my morning tea as the Florida panhandle prepared for a direct hit from Hurricane Opal. Also on that day a jury was ready to acquit O.J. It was that same afternoon I attended a funeral of an old dear friend. A man loved by so many. A man who was an uncle to me and others.

His nephews, sons and daughter grew up with me. This was Buster's uncle, the friend who saw me in Vietnam just before he left for home. I hadn't seen Buster for many years and I knew he'd be there.

"Damn I hate funerals," I said to myself. My stomach was in knots and my old friend the headache had joined me again. I had a recurring nightmare about a funeral, and it made me phobic about them.

In the nightmare, I dream I'm at Bunny's funeral. Bunny's in a coffin and I'm being dragged up to see him. I kick and scream, not wanting to see him. I get closer and peek in. There's a body dressed in a dress green Army uniform. Just the body. No head.

My last memory of Bunny in the real world was a body without a head. Even now, I can't remember what Bunny looked like. The traumatic moment must have shocked my system. Women who witnessed the killing fields of Cambodia were known to have lost their eyesight over watching their loved ones murdered. Maybe that was me. I hadn't lost my eyesight, just Bunny's face.

But as the hurricane approached that day I could only

think of a man we all called uncle Fibber. A big man with a heart of gold. A man who said he couldn't read but had to be one of the smartest men I ever knew. He will be missed and there will never be another like him.

At the viewing the night before the funeral I couldn't walk up to his body, but I could see it from a distance. Just one glance is all I could do. In my mind I had a certain way I wanted to remember him. That was all right for me. He would understand.

Buster walked in looking a little older than I remembered. We hugged. We talked some before he went over to his aunt in the front row. Confronting his aunt was a difficult thing for him to do. Buster loved his uncle so much and I choked back the tears as I watched him embrace her.

The next day was fairly calm. The turbulent winds swirled out in the Gulf of Mexico only a hundred miles from us. Hurricane Opal raced toward the Florida panhandle. You couldn't feel it though, in our west coast town—the town where Fibber was born and raised.

"Look at all these cars," I said to Kathy as we pulled into the small neighborhood cemetery only blocks from our house.

"Everyone loved Fibber," she said, her eyes red from crying.

"That's how you determine wealth," I said.

"What do you mean?" asked Kathy.

"The friends you've made over the years are what counts. It doesn't matter how much money you have; it's how you were loved while you were here."

Kathy smiled and agreed.

As we walked to the grave sight on that overcast day I looked around. The air had a familiar scent to it. Something that I recalled from my youth. All of a sudden things were changing around me. I glanced at faces of people I hadn't seen for years. I realized these were the people I'd known while growing up. Our lives had touched and now we were back together again. I didn't have this confused messed up feeling with me that day. The day was set aside from all that was going on in the world. Our little section of the world was protected from the hassles of the trial of the century, war in Bosnia, the hurricane, or anything.

As they lowered the casket I looked to the gray, slow-moving clouds. For a moment the sun peeked through.

I smiled. For a moment there was peace, and I said goodbye. Our little section of town felt as it had thirty years ago. It was a good feeling to know a friend was put to rest, no longer in pain. He would have loved the way people spoke of him as they showed their respects.

It seemed natural to me, and for the first time in years, I realized that although saying goodbye was hard, I wanted to say goodbye to others that I never had the chance to. It seemed attending Fibber's funeral was a way to deal with others' deaths. Accepting loss was part of the healing process, yet it was something I could never do before. Would saying goodbye to Fibber be a start?

That night I had a Vet Center meeting.

"I went to a funeral," I said.

All in the room became quiet and all eyes were fixed on me. No vet liked funerals.

"I had to go. This guy was special."

"How did you handle it?" asked the counselor, another 'Nam vet.

"Hard, but I saw the light."

The counselor's eyebrows went up. "In what way, Phil?"

"Well, I was with friends I grew up with. I realized their lives have been going on while mine has been stuck in this damn time machine. Life will go on with or without us."

"You're right," said the counselor.

Others nodded their heads in agreement. Some sat with a

dead stare. I knew why; they hadn't reached the point yet where they could accept certain deaths. Each must find his own bend in the road that will take him to a better life. It was something everyone in the room sought.

Was I finally at a point in my life to accept Vietnam? Maybe, but I was still plagued by the anger. If I were to forget it all, would I have to admit the war had been fought in vain?

I wasn't ready for that; I never would be.

What I was ready for was saying goodbye to brave young men who I had the honor to serve with. This was the time to start. I wanted to believe the war was wrong but at the same time, I needed a reason for the deaths of my buddies.

"If you can get yourself to attend a funeral of a friend, then maybe it can help you," I said.

Maria, the Vet Center doctor, smiled at me. "That's right," she said. "Maybe it could."

The meeting closed with a discussion of the uncertain future of the Vet Center. Budget cuts seemed imminent. There was talk of employees being put on leave. There would be a lot of changes in the next few months.

The next morning I met with Maria. After three years I felt a change coming on. Maybe it was time for me to leave for a while.

"So, what's going on with you?" she asked, genuine concern in her voice.

"I don't know. Maybe I should stop coming every week. Could use a break."

"I think that might be a good idea. You've come a long way."

"I don't want to start another group session with all new guys. I don't want to bring up all the memories again," I said.

"I agree, but we're here for you. Anytime you want to come back you can."

"Thanks, I appreciate that. It's good to know if I slip I

have the Vet Center," I said.

I still had my monthly session with Joe and appointments at the VA hospital. Most importantly I had the friends I'd made at the Vet Center. We were like a chain you couldn't break. I left the Vet Center feeling a little sad and a little happy. 'Nam was still there as I glanced at the pictures and Vietnam map on the wall. I saw the 9th Division patch affixed in the glass showcase hanging over the fireplace in the meeting room.

"Chain, Chain, Chain! Chain of fools!" Aretha Franklin sang in my mind, as I placed myself back with the 9th. It was hot and muddy. We were pulling ourselves through the thick mud like men on a chain gang, Working together, relying on one another. Keep the chain strong; never break a link. But sometimes we lost a link and it would screw up the whole damn chain.

No sweat, because someone was always there to fill the missing link. A FNG. Never the one to fill the shoes of the guy before him until he broke his cherry—shot a Viet Cong, helped you in a time of need, or he too got blown away. One thing was for sure; he learned to be there. He learned to be part of the chain. Was I now breaking the chain? I didn't want to feel I was. I wanted to be there if needed by a fellow vet.

What would be ahead for me? No one could answer that one but me. I wasn't even sure what I was looking for anymore—happiness, maybe—but I knew with the courage and strength I learned from Vietnam, I was sure I'd find it.

Chapter Twenty-Two

JOE ADCOCK MADE a promise to himself years ago. As a veteran readjustment counselor he knew first hand the importance of closure, and of recognition. When the Vietnam Veterans Memorial in DC was built, he knew he had to take as many veterans there as he could.

Building The Wall was the first step in a healing process for many. It gave people a chance to grieve for lost loved ones and it showed people cared for those who paid the ultimate sacrifice. Joe felt very lucky to return home from Vietnam and he made a life-long commitment to serve other veterans. He kept his vow, and I was one of the lucky ones to have Joe as a counselor.

The trip was in the works for over a year before the date was set. The trip would be on Veteran's Day in 1997. We'd go by train, and several women who served as nurses in Vietnam would join us. That in itself carried deep meeting to us who where wounded in Vietnam. We held our nurses, our angels, in high regards.

Joe was also involved in the initial creation of the Vet Centers. The Vet Centers were started by the vets themselves to help their brothers readjust to civilian life after the war. Most had nowhere to turn and they needed a safe place to talk to about their war experiences. Most vets had hid their feelings like they had with their uniforms—stuff them away in a closet and forget about them. Vets would only feel comfortable with other vets so they needed a place that was not connected to the VA system, a system that back then turned their backs on veterans needing help because they served in Vietnam.

I had been one of those veterans they had abandoned. I had concealed my emotions, but that first trip to the Moving Wall unleashed over twenty years of deep-seated emotions that haunted my soul. Now I had a chance to actually go to Washington to see the permanent Wall—the dedication to my comrades, the sacred ground where our heroes stood for all to see. My emotions stirred as I anticipated the trip. I wasn't alone.

Twenty of us signed up for the trip. Joe asked me if I'd like to share a room with him and another vet. I was honored that Joe had asked me. We shared a connection.

There was a chill in the air when we all arrived at the bus terminal in Pinellas Park, Florida. I liked that. I was tired of the hot, humid weather and looked forward to an autumn in DC. It had been years since I'd experienced the changing of the leaves.

The bus trip took us to Orlando where we left on the train. It was a long day and the train was late. It reminded me of the Army already. Traveling together and joking. Hurrying up, just to wait. It was after five before we actually left Orlando and started the twenty-plus hour trip to Washington DC.

Just like in the Army, I didn't remember falling asleep. We didn't have cabins on the train so we had to nap in our chairs. We also made frequent trips to the dining car for food and snacks. Some guys just stayed in there and talked all night. I think most had The Wall on their minds and wondered how they'd react when they finally faced it. I know I did.

I thought a lot as I glanced out the window of that train. I watched the countryside and towns that dotted it as we sped past. I wondered how many were on The Wall from the towns I peeked at. It seemed fitting to travel by train. We saw America as we headed north to honor the heroes that fought for the little towns and villages I was looking at. I thought of my friends and smiled. They would have been proud they built a monument of such great importance for them.

We arrived in DC and rented several vans to take us to our hotel which would be within walking distance of The Wall. By the time we arrived at the hotel, a hush settled over us. Everyone seemed to go off into our own little worlds as we had in Vietnam. Each had their own personal stories and sentiments about the war, but we all had one thing in common. We each knew someone on that wall.

It was almost dark before a handful of us ventured off to The Wall. As we approached a path close to the entrance, we were still. It was as if we were on patrol.

My chest tightened and my heart beat faster as I glanced ahead and saw the infamous long black wall. Lights beamed up from the ground, towards the panels. A light rain misted the wall, causing it to glimmer.

We stopped in front of the monument, reluctant to approach. I looked at the ground and saw items of many different kinds sitting in front of the names etched in stone. Poems, letters, pictures, old caps, flowers, Boy Scout badges, and more were propped up against the memorial.

When I saw boyhood mementos, the words "momma's own, names etched in stone" hit me.

I walked up. I touched a name and I prayed. I touched another. I had a song in my head, and by the time I went to bed that night I had written a song called "Touching Your Name."

We all comforted one another. Larry, the severely wounded Marine medic, fell apart in front of me. This tough-looking, hardened warrior put on a good facade. His emotions overwhelmed him and he broke down, collapsing in my arms. Years of holding it back were gone.

And we were there for him as he once was as a medic for his buddies. He paid a big price for his country, yet he knew the ones on that Wall were the heroes we all must honor forever. His own stories about the war were still with him, locked in his mind forever. So were mine. I knew each man on that Wall had a personal connection with me.

I held their names against the palms of my hands, feeling the cold, slick marble. I cried, so confused. I was still angry, but also hurt and filled with sorrow. At the same time I felt fortunate, not only to be alive to honor the men on The Wall, but to have known the heroes whose names were listed there.

The air was crisp, yet damp. I shivered. I felt so lonely. I though of girlfriends and wives whose loved ones hadn't returned. It must have hurt them so much. I was lucky. I remembered coming home, and nothing was sweeter than to hold your girl close again, hopefully forever. It didn't happen for the 58,000 men on The Wall, but for many veterans, coming home didn't mean forever either. Over forty percent of male Vietnam veterans ended up divorced.

The next day we walked over early. People swarmed the monument, each approaching in their own way.

One old man stood back and he cried. "Why?" he said. "What a waste."

I needed to say something to him. I put a hand on his shoulder and said, "Turn around, old soldier. Take a look. They didn't die in vain."

He smiled with tears in his eyes. He nodded.

I didn't know who he knew on that wall, but I think he walked away feeling better, or at least putting some closure to that part of his life.

I learned eight female Army nurses were on The Wall. The only women. I called them "Eight Lovely Angels On A Wall" and it became the next song I would write about my trip to DC. I also used the line "Turn around, old soldier, take a look." It fit. So did the leaves of many colors that I enjoyed looking at that day. To me, they were the color of America. In battle there was no color barrier. I saw comrades hug all day long—black, white, Indian—it didn't matter. The bond was there and it remained strong.

The last day at The Wall was Veteran's Day. Emmy Lou Harris was the guest singer on stage. She sang about America with a feeling that the war personally touched her. She introduced a young singer named Jamie O'Hara. He did a song called "50,000 Names" that had us all crying that day.

I left feeling somewhat cleansed. Not fully, but it felt good to finally get the chance to grieve among others who understood what I felt. Together we would heal each other. We appreciated each other and we saw how other Americans appreciated us. That alone meant so much to us. Recognition was way overdue.

Someone had a vision to build that wall. Jan Scruggs, a Vietnam veteran himself, knew we needed a monument for our fallen Vietnam veterans. It would be instrumental in helping thousands of Americans where were touched by the war.

I saw Jan Scruggs standing near The Wall that last day. I walked over and thanked him and shook his hand. We posed for a picture together.

The trip to The Wall started a healing process for me, and I hoped, for others. The trip back on the train was long. We were so tired and sleeping sitting up was impossible. But my thoughts of the weekend were still with me and I couldn't wait to share my experience with Kathy and Michelle.

And I couldn't wait to get my guitar and put words to chords. I made arrangements with a singer/guitarist friend of mine named Devon Anderson to help me out in a studio. We did a five-song CD—four by me, and one by Devon: "Joe Plays His Guitar."

My first song was "Eight Angels on a Wall." After I learned of the eight women, Army nurses that were killed in Vietnam and being the only women on the wall, I wrote about them. I spent a day at The Wall and looked around at the people. I wrote "Angels on a Wall," also about my feelings of the day.

I wrote one dedicated to a girl who lost her dad. Her dad's name is on the same panel as some of my friends. I saw a graduation notice and a note she left for her dad at the foot of the panel. I bent down and read the letter and saw she was to graduate the same college my daughter was attending. I saw also that she was majoring in education, as was my daughter. I wrote about her and dedicated the song to the Sons and Daughters In Touch program, a program set up to help people find friends of their lost love ones.

I wrote "Touching Your Name" about that first night at The Wall. The last song was about my last day in Vietnam. A soldier on the Mekong Delta on his last day inspired "Mekong River, I'm Going Home." Instead of looking at the river as a place of horror from war, I looked at it as a thing of beauty and peacefulness and prayed for one more day so I could make it home to my wife.

When I released my CD, many veterans seemed to want copies. I was glad my words were touching others.

I'll always be thankful for Joe Adcock inviting me to The Wall. And when I was there I had a bracelet made for him with his name and Marine insignia on it.

When Joe retired, Jimmy, my veteran friend from the 4th Division and I gave him a case we had made with a Purple Heart medal in it. The words inscribe in the case said, "You gave us your heart, we give you ours." He was touched to tears.

Chapter Twenty-Three

I WAS ADJUSTING the best I could after I received my award letter but Vietnam is not an easy memory to shake. The memories brought to surface through my struggles took a toll on my health and on my marriage. I didn't see it coming, but as many of my Vietnam veteran comrades, I fell through the cracks. I became another statistic. I was just another victim of the war and I carried all the dirty baggage that went along with it.

I realized my participation in the war affected not only my health but my marriage as well. With that I still hold a lot of pain. I never wanted to hurt the woman who loved me so much, but that's what happened. My wife was always there for me, and God only knows what I would have done without her support. She saw me through the rough times in war and at home. Our love ran deep and true, but I learned the hard way—even good things can end.

Around the time of my thirtieth high school class reunion a change was coming. I had been an average student and fairly popular, but was never involved in many school activities. For some strange reason I felt a need to be on the reunion committee this time. At the reunion committee meeting someone suggested that a tribute to Vietnam veterans should be included in the weekend's activities. I was surprised and instantly felt I was the person who should say something to honor my comrades.

But I wasn't alone; there were three other Vietnam vets on the committee. When they discovered I was a wounded veteran, all eyes were on me to come up with a short program honoring our veterans. I agreed to write something. I was told to keep it around five minutes.

I could tell others on the committee were nervous that I'd just praise the veteran and maybe try and complain about our treatment after returning home. But that's not what I had in mind. That night I couldn't sleep so I worked on a speech—a speech that I wanted someone else to read. I never could give a speech and never had the confidence to do anything like this before. The subject matter was closer to my heart than I'd ever realized. Once I started to write the words came easy—from the heart. It was important for everyone to feel good about what I was going to write.

It was a difficult time for us in the class of 1968. Some went to war and some didn't. I needed to make it all fit into my speech. It was a reunion to reflect on our time as seniors entering a confused and troubled world. We all had dreams and hopes of a bright future but we all knew that for some Vietnam was in that future.

It was late into the night as I typed my speech. Kathy peeked in often to check on me.

"You still writing? I can't believe you're going to give a speech."

"Well, maybe. I think I'll write it and let someone else read it," I said.

"Let me read it after you're done, okay?"

"Sure, I'll be done in a few. I have five pages and it might be too long."

"They only want a five minute speech? That's going to be hard to do," said Kathy.

"I know, but if they trust me they'll let me have more time."

In a few minutes I was done. I printed it out and surprised myself on how fast I had prepared the speech. I looked it over and handed it to Kathy. She stood in the bedroom doorway and read it. Her eyes welled up with tears. It was hitting home with her. She too was from the class of 1968.

"Wow! This is good. But there's one thing," she said.

"What's that?"

"Only one person can deliver this speech," she said, "and that's you."

My tears joined hers and we hugged. Vietnam was so close to the surface for both of us. The scars were deep. I needed to give that speech as much as others needed to hear it. The class .of 1968 needed to heal.

The next week I brought the speech to the meeting. I let the other veterans read it. I instantly had their approval to deliver the speech. The chairman of the committee was hesitant about the length of the speech but was convinced I'd do my best to keep it short. I told her it would be about ten minutes but knew it would last about twenty. I also trusted that once I had the room's attention, the length wouldn't matter.

We decided to set up a table with pictures and items of the time period. Some brought in medals, one brought a sword, and others brought in pictures. The display was to be set up along a table of other memorabilia.

The speech was written two months before the reunion. That gave me enough time to practice delivering it and remembering it. But I was still nervous. I worried about the reaction. Our class had been divided. There were war protestors, some that served, some that went off to college and some who didn't bother with either. There were also some who went to college for one purpose that was to avoid the draft. Those were the ones who probably had the guilt and they were the ones who wondered how it was over there. Regardless of what one's beliefs were back then, the speech would be a message to all.

As I waited for the reunion, my lieutenant was in contact

with me. He said he was writing for me to receive the Bronze Star that he felt I deserved. Others too supported me and wrote letters about me getting the Star.

Tom Veit, a retired major who had served with the 9th Division, took a concern and led a charge for one of his own to receive the long-awaited medal.

"We take care of our own," he had said. He cared for his comrades. It made me realize how dedicated some officers were toward their men. The paperwork was in and then it slipped my mind. After a couple of rejections because of no records, I figured it would never happen. At the time I was to get the award in 1970 I didn't care. I had the Purple Heart, but others lost their lives and were wounded seriously. I figured my medal was my life and making it out of the 'Nam.

With all the attention I was receiving, Kathy stood silent. Her memories of Vietnam were as horrible as mine. When I was wounded she didn't know how bad or even if I would survive. It wasn't until she received a letter from me a week later that she knew I was all right. Then we were deceived in believing I'd be sent home because of the head wound. But that never happened. I finished my year in Vietnam, though sick and in pain. She could never forgive the government for what they did to her husband. And she could never accept the way the VA treated those in need who had to fight for benefits. When it came down to it, she too was a veteran of the lousy war. Wives who had to deal with sick husbands from war need to get their own medals and maybe someday they will. But bringing up my past hurt her and I never realized it.

The reunion date was getting nearer. I had the speech well memorized by the time August 1998 came around. The speech would be at the Saturday night dinner and dance. We had the reunion at the Belleview Biltmore Hotel in Bellaire, Florida. The hotel is the largest wooden structure in the world and overlooks the bay toward Clearwater Beach on the Gulf of

Mexico. It's in an area of high-priced homes and a beautiful golf course.

We pulled up to the hotel around midday that Friday afternoon. We went with another couple, Linda and Bob. Linda and her bother Wally grew up in the house in back of ours. We stayed friends. Bob is a police officer and worked in a small beach town close to the VA Hospital. He would often pick up veterans that were disorderly and drunk. He'd try and talk with them and also would drive them for help to the hospital. Many times the veteran would be turned away and Bob would take the guy back to the beach and get them a cup of coffee. He became a friend to many veterans on his beat.

We signed in for two nights and made our way to our rooms. We passed old friends in the lobby, stopping to talk to some. It was so good to see friends from so long ago. The faces would look familiar but couldn't quite make them all out until the nametags were in place that night. I played guitar and sang at the cocktail party that night. I couldn't believe I had the nerve to do that. But I did it to give me more courage to deliver the speech the next night. It helped, the music went over well and people were friendly toward me.

That afternoon before the speech I had a headache and became very nervous. Kathy told me to take a hot bath and try to relax, so I did.

"I hope they like the speech. Man, why did I say I'd do it?"

"Because it's time and you need to do it, that's why," said Kathy.

"I know, but now I remember so many were against the war back then. Besides, I never gave a speech. I had speech in my senior year and barely passed. I almost didn't graduate because of that speech class."

"You're kidding?"

"Yeah, I hated it and would always be absent the day of

my speeches. I was told to make the remainder of the speeches and I needed to pull a C to make it."

"Well this time you are ready and you are dealing with a subject you feel strongly about. I have faith in you."

"Thanks, I needed that. Think the bath water is ready. I took a pain pill and it's starting to work," I said.

I went into the bathroom and lowered myself into the old bathtub. The room had high ceilings and the woodwork and wallpaper was of Victorian style. I lay back and felt the warm water surround my body. I started counting the ceiling tiles and kept dunking the washcloth into the hot water and putting it across my eyes. The headache was easing and my thoughts went back to my youth. I smiled again. I could do this. I had hated speaking in public in high school, but now I had a chance to do something good. I would face my fear and say my piece.

I was still a soldier in my mind when I found myself standing in front of two hundred and fifty fellow classmates to prove what we did was just. I wanted respect for me and my fellow comrades. I had my dead buddies in my mind as well. Their spirits lifted me toward that podium that night. The words seemed to flow easily. I felt as though another person was talking, but it was me. I had the confidence I lacked as a youth and it felt good.

Jim Drain, another Vietnam veteran, went up before me. He recited a short poem he wrote about what it felt like during that time of war and confusion. Then he introduced me.

"It gives me great honor and a privilege to introduce to you a decorated Vietnam veteran wounded during the spring offensive in Cambodia. Your fellow classmate, Phil Ferrazano."

The class let out whistles and hollers and clapped long and hard. I was in shock. They already respected me as a Vietnam veteran. Most already gave me approval before I even delivered the speech. I smiled and stood, turned toward the crowd and waved. I glanced at my wife and she smiled at me. Our eyes met and I could tell she felt proud. I made my way to the stage and asked the crowd to quiet it down. I knew I had to do my best and make myself worthy of the applause. It was time.

"I know the subject of the Vietnam War is not easy to talk about," I began, "but it was part of our history and there are over 58,000 reasons why we should never forget. I'm proud that our class of 1968 thought it was time we recognize those who served our country. I feel honored to have the opportunity to speak a few words for myself and my comrades, and those whose lives were touched in anyway, by the Vietnam War.

"By 1968 I think most opposed the war. We know that some volunteered and some served against their will. No matter. Once called, all served with honor and all became emotionally attached to that war.

"Vietnam to us, played hell on the mind. You were pulled between an obligation to your country, the American tradition, and what you believed was morally right. Vietnam was a difficult time for all of us.

"On Valentines Day 1970, there were four of us from Clearwater that landed in Vietnam. We hung together like lost puppies away from home. We were sent to the headquarters company for the 9th Infantry Division for orientation and to be told that some of us wouldn't make it home.

"After a few days we were separated and sent to different units. My last night at that headquarters company I walked guard duty around a building. On one side of the building there were caskets set up to be sent home. Every time I got to the side of the building with the caskets I couldn't help to look. I couldn't stop thinking what may lie ahead of me in my one-year tour of duty. Would I even make the year?

"I glanced at the stars that night with tears rolling down my face. That night I truly realized the party was over. My youth would be something in my past. I thought of my wife of only two months, my family and friends and I thought of myself. What kind of person was I? Did I have it in me to be a soldier? How would I react when called upon? What would I do when faced against the enemy? Would I be wounded or killed? Sadly these fears were becoming reality. Each event building to the ultimate climax when I almost died. You'd think dying was my greatest fear. I felt close to God so I didn't fear it. You get religion real fast in a foxhole. I can remember at that time being very tired and worn out, both physically and mentally. It was confusing at home. My family received word I was wounded to the head without knowing if I was all right. This was one week before my younger brother graduated from the class of nineteen seventy. Prayers echoed the halls of CHS for me.

"It was confusing for us too in Vietnam. We first figured we were there to win a war. It turned out to be a battle for you and your buddies to survive. We felt alone in our struggles and depended on each other. We were sick of all the politicians back home that wouldn't do a thing to stop the war. The same ones that would turn down bills for veteran benefits. The same ones who found ways for their sons to avoid the draft.

"I hated the war, the endless miserable rainy nights, the feelings of worthlessness and loneliness. The wondering if your next step would be your last and the empty feeling you got when you watched a buddy die. Please don't tell me of government policy and betrayal. Don't tell me what it was like in Vietnam. My comrades and I can tell you.

"I was wounded on May 26, 1970 during the Cambodian invasion. We as infantry soldiers feared and had our doubts about going into Cambodia. Many times we stood and refused certain orders we knew were unsafe. We had a saying: 'What could they do to us? Draft us? Put us in the infantry and send us to Vietnam?'

"Back home all were celebrating Memorial Day weekend while I was experiencing the true meaning of it first hand.

"It was around four in the morning when we were attacked by a large, well trained, NVA force. Mortars landed on my position and altered the way I would live the rest of my life, forever. I lay wounded; fighting for my life while the NVA started an aggressive ground assault. Two friends next to me were dead one of whom I had just changed places with. He was a father with four kids. He told me that night he decided not to stay in service, as did others in his family.

"A few years ago one of his daughters phoned me. She wanted to know something about the dad she never knew. She always believed he died in a plane crash. I said, 'No, he died on the ground next to me, a hero, believing he was doing the right thing.'

"That early morning, half of my company was wiped out. That's when every ounce of youth and innocents I was trying to savor was finally gone. I even felt somewhat peaceful for a moment. But the horror continued when our choppers were loaded full with men crying, "Oh God!" and asking for their mothers. The faces I saw in that mash unit will always be branded in my mind. I refused to die because I was loved by my wife, family and friends and God. God played a big part and there were reasons why he spared me. I see one reason every time I look at my young daughter. Also I had to give this speech at my 30th class reunion.

"Yes, I know the meaning of guilt and the feeling of what it was like to say 'Why him and not me?' There's never an answer why some go to war and some don't. For this I say, if you didn't go, please don't feel guilt. You can be proud of what you stood for at that difficult time in your young lives. Many still hurt over the way we were treated in Vietnam. Especially for the wounded who today still endure continued health problems. I still resent those who turn a cheek and say "Oh well forget about it, that was a long time ago." I guess that's easy to say unless your family was affected by the Vietnam War.

"Our war was like no other. Most went over alone and returned alone. We slipped back into society and tried to forget the war. We also had no one to talk to about it so we hid our emotions and went on listening to others who knew all about Vietnam, even though they had never even been there.

"We as returning veterans heard all the comments. 'How many people did you shoot?' 'You didn't have to go you know.' 'You fought for nothing.' Comments that proved to me that those my age were still very naive about what Vietnam was really like.

"I've encountered many thoughtful people who showed me sincere respect for what myself and my comrades endured. And we, by some, were labeled as losers of a very unpopular war. We in battle didn't lose the war. It was lost here by the politicians and those who knew they wouldn't have to send their sons into the hellhole we called the 'Nam.

"Does Vietnam ever cross my mind? Yes, I can honestly say it does, a lot of times. It's only natural—a young man right out of high school cannot be thrown into a horrible situation such as war and not be affected. But it's because of Vietnam that I'm able to stand before you tonight, confident. Most Vietnam veterans have been able to face all their challenges in life head on. The Vietnam experience taught us well how to survive and taught us that we could accomplish anything we really wanted to. Most Vietnam veterans have become successful in business and in life. Contrary to many beliefs, the Vietnam veteran is a caring person who loves his family, country and life. A person who enjoys the simple treasures in life that most take for granted.

"Sometimes I think back of who I once was, and think of those who died. I wonder what they could have been. Yes they cross my mind. I get sad and at times I smile, because you see, men in battle get very close to each other. William Shakespeare wrote almost four hundred years ago, 'We few, we happy few, we band of brothers. For he today who sheds his blood with me shall be my brother.' Words of so long ago still hold true today.

"When it was brought up at a reunion committee meeting that someone suggested we honor those out of this class who served in the military, I quickly felt a connection and a desire to be the one to say something. I felt it important to myself and my comrades to express the real emotional feelings about a difficult period in our young lives.

"I speak these words not for any recognition to myself, but for all in here to understand some feelings of those who served. Though some didn't serve in battle, they too were ready. They gave a big part of themselves in a very unselfish way. Some made the military a career, and for this we say, thank you for your service.

"In 1968 we all had our opinions on what was right or wrong about the war. That doesn't matter now. We all lived with fear, in our teen years that one would go to Vietnam if one didn't stay in school. We learned early on we were entering a cruel world. Martin Luther King was assassinated, and days before we graduated, it was Bobby Kennedy. In 1968 we were told we had a handle on the war. That changed with the attacks during Tet when the Vietcong infiltrated into Saigon and launched attacks all through cities and towns we thought were safe. In 1968 we lost our beloved Frank Russell to cancer. And in 1968 a fun-loving kid quit cruising Steak 'n Shake with his friend Wally in his '55 caddy because he met his future wife one warm summer night on Clearwater Beach. And it was that year for many of us that Vietnam hit home. Jimmy Lewis was killed in Vietnam. Jimmy was killed not even two months in country. I can still remember Joking with him in Mr. Sackett's music class. A few days ago he would have turned fifty. I know he'd be proud that I'm talking about him. Guess you can say he's one of our forever-young heroes. I touched his name on The Wall in Washington, DC, last November. Panel 37W, line 57. I touched many names that day, all heroes.

"I want to believe those on The Wall died for a purpose and the lessons learned by Vietnam are the reasons we didn't let them die in vain. The way we go into battle now has changed because of Vietnam. Never again will our young—our children—fight with their hands tied. Never again will we as a nation—as a people—let a war divide us. Never again will our young go to war without full support. Those are the reasons why some of my friends grace that infamous long black wall in Washington, DC.

"Classmates, I've just taken you on an emotional roller coaster ride. That is what Vietnam was all about. It tugged at your deepest emotions and hit all your senses, many times over until you became numb. Sadly for some, that numbness has never left.

"Yes, we've all faced difficult times. For some it was Vietnam. Today I can't say I regret serving there. The reason, because of the ones I served with. I feel privileged to have served with fine, brave young men, from all parts of the country who sacrificed it all for their beliefs and their country. Some died believing we would only win the war. As a youth we had our beliefs and we never stopped believing and dreaming. We can all be proud of what this class of 1968 has accomplished. Those who ever experienced battle would never wish battle on anyone. So, no one should ever feel guilt for not serving. What would be nice is for all to show respect to those who did. I feel this class, as always, has decided to be the leader among classes and honor those who served.

"We've come a long way in thirty years. We've dedicated ourselves to raising our families, working hard and serving our communities. Be proud. We've done what was expected of us and more. We've made our mark; we are America. To live as Americans as we do, we have to thank those who gave for our country and those who ever wore a uniform, in peacetime or no—any branch of the service.

"The Vietnam veteran was probably the last warrior of his kind. Your generation's warrior—the so-called, hippy generation warrior. Well let me say, I saw how that hippy generation fought and died. You can be proud. They were brave and courageous as any before them.

"Freedom is not free, it comes with a price. I appreciate that my class wanted to stand and say thanks to those who served. I hope my words did speak for all here tonight. I would like all vets right now, who served their country to stand. It's been a long time, but now I can honestly say we were welcomed home. God bless us all. I'm a proud veteran, holder of the Purple Heart Medal. But tonight, I'm most proud to be your fellow class of 1968 classmate. Thank you."

The speech ended. Not a sound in the room, and then suddenly, an overwhelming standing ovation. I saw tears in some as they came up to me to shake my hand.

Before I left the stage one classmate ran to me and grabbed my hand and said, "John Kennedy was my hero and you sounded just like him."

I was floored. I still don't know where that voice came from, but I'm sure I had help from somewhere. People thanked me for freeing them. The ones who missed Vietnam where just as happy I gave the speech as the veterans. I had achieved far more than I ever anticipated.

"That speech took you thirty years to write," one classmate said.

"I wish I could hold an audience in the palms of my hands like you did," said another, a lawyer.

"Anytime you need anything for a veteran's organization, donations, whatever, I'll be there," said the senior class president, a doctor.

Our class football hero, with tears in his eyes hugged me and said, "I thought I was the hero, but you're the real hero. Thank you for what you did."

After the reunion the flood of appreciation didn't stop. The comments, phone calls, and emails came in throughout the year. Two parents whose sons were killed in Vietnam called me. Their sons attended Clearwater High. "Before your speech, nobody had done anything at the reunions to honor our boys," they said. "Thank you, and God bless." Calls like those were the hardest to take, but they were also the most meaningful.

The newspaper ran a whole page story about me for Veteran's Day and told how I recorded a music CD honoring veterans. The CD was put on a web page and people would contact me after they read about my music. Many Vietnam veterans would contact me after they heard and read my words that honored them and those who were on The Wall.

One day I received an email from someone who was in the 9th Division. He had been in my unit, but a year earlier. He wanted to find the person who last owned the company guitar. There were four owners. He had found three. It had been a puzzle for him for years.

I told him the guitar had been lost in a fire. With that email he was able to locate the last owner of the famed guitar that was handed down through the years. That last owner was me. And he learned the story of how it was destroyed. It would have gone home that year with me because the 9th was going home. A piece of history went up in smoke. The guitar, as an old soldier preformed its tour of duty, but like so many of us, it never made it home. It served its purpose and died.

Later the story of the 9th Division guitar was immortalized in Lee Andresen's book *Battle Notes: Music Of The Vietnam War*.

All the attention I was getting brought Vietnam back, but

in a different way this time. People were finally showing they cared about what my comrades and I had gone through. The praise was way overdue.

Unfortunately, my life was about to change once more. This time it would be more devastating than any mortar shell, tougher than any jungle, and more painful than lying in that Quonset hut waiting for the doctors to dig hot scraps of metal from my skin.

I had made it out of the mucky swamps of Vietnam. I had stood on that stage and listened to the praise of my peers. But now I was about to tumble back into the quagmire. I was the hero—but I heard it once said, "Show me a hero and I'll show you a tragedy." The words rang all too true for me, and my wife.

Chapter Twenty-Four

WHILE I WAS IN the limelight, my wife stood in the shadows. I felt guilty because she had endured the Vietnam trip also—not only the waiting for me to return home, but the health issues that came later down the road. My mistreatment by the VA took a toll on her as well. She hated the way I had to beg for treatment, and when I did get treatment it usually was lousy.

The stress we endured together contributed to the deterioration of what we at one time had—a good, loving, and trusting marriage. It was very hard to handle when it all came apart.

A new year was approaching: the millennium. The big two thousand. The year of new beginnings and new goals. The year we had it made. Our daughter would turn twenty-one, graduate college, and get married. The plan was falling in place and we both seemed happy, but it was the calm before the storm. The battle was about to heat up and my survival techniques once again would be tested to the limit.

Our daughter was busy with her own life now. We'd go out more with friends, but the attention always seemed focused on me. My speech at the reunion and my CD honoring veterans garnered me some great positive attention. There was also some noise about me being nominated for the Bronze Star, after all this time.

As always, Kathy stood in the shadows. The interest others seemed to have in me drove a wedge between us. She once said people saw me as a hero, that I could do no wrong. Of course,

she knew better. After all that I had put her through, I didn't
feel like any hero.

✪ ✪ ✪

NEW YEARS EVE, 1999 was a colder than any other I could
remember. Florida winters are usually mild but this night was
cold, with a wet air that cut right to the bone. It would prove to
be the coldest day of my life.

That night we met friends at an Italian restaurant for a
quiet evening to bring in the new year. Kathy sat quiet most of
the night as we all talked and joked and enjoyed our meal. I
sensed something was wrong.

"Let's go to the tiki bar," she said. "The guys are playing."

"It's too cold," I said. "And it's raining."

"You're a party pooper," she said.

"Fine, fine...we'll go." I wasn't happy about it at all.
Looking back, I think she wanted to go to break away from the
rest of our friends.

Outside the rain was light but once at the bar it stopped.
The air was crisp and starting to clear up. We didn't talk, just
sat back and listened to the music.

Fifteen minutes before midnight, I finally got tired of the
uncomfortable silence.

"What the hell's the matter?" I asked. "You've been quiet
all night."

"I know we've been married a long time, and this is hard,"
Kathy said.

"What?" I asked with a fear in my voice and a knot in my
stomach.

"I don't want to hurt you..."

"What are you talking about?"

The music suddenly seemed distant, as if my world had
been dropped into a fog.

"I want out."

"What the hell do you mean, 'you want out'?"

"I know it's hard, but I've been giving it a lot of thought. We're both turning fifty this year. Is this all there is?" she asked.

"Are you kidding me?" I bellowed. "You're leaving me right before midnight on New Years Eve?"

Her expression hardened. My uncontrolled anger seemed to make her more resolute.

"Please, just go," she said. "I know what I'm doing. I'll get a ride home."

My face went numb. My life suddenly seemed worthless and bare—empty.

Bewildered, I left. Got into the car and went about a block and then made a hard, fast u-turn. I couldn't accept what was happening to us. Not after all this time.

I walked back to the outside bar but instead jumped a low wall adjacent to the tiki bar's property. I found myself in wet grass up to my ass. The delta was my first thought. It seemed that the 'Nam always played through my head during the most horrible moments of my life.

As midnight neared, I watched Kathy circulate through the party, talking to others as if nothing had happened. For the first time since Vietnam, I was going to be alone on New Years Eve. When I had returned from 'Nam, we had promised each other we'd always be together at the start of each new year.

2000 was supposed to be a year filled with milestones— our daughter's college graduation, our fiftieth birthdays, and a new independence that would finally allow us to spend time together.

Instead, I was alone.

Bursts of red, green and blue fireworks light up the sky over the bay. The booms and pops pulled me back to Vietnam. I was in another battle. This one wounded me more than shrapnel that ripped through my back—this one took another piece of my heart. People kissed and hugged the new year in. For the first time since 'Nam I wasn't there to kiss my wife.

A month went by and we tried to work our problems out, but although we could get along, we couldn't resolve our differences. Her mind was made up and I was reliving what my parents had gone through when I was twenty-four. I hurt then and I knew how it would hurt Michelle.

Joe had me come in weekly, sometimes every day, until I calmed down. At one session Joe suggested I just give her some space, her own independence.

"Joe, she comes and goes as she likes."

"It's not about that. She needs to be her own person. Does she have her own car?" he asked.

"We have only one now. When I closed the business we sold my truck."

"Well, get another truck and just let her have the car for herself again."

"Yeah, I'll do anything. But I think it's more than that."

"Don't give up on her that easy, man she's been through a lot with you."

"I know, that's probably the problem. All the 'Nam stuff." I sat and put my hands to my face, constantly rubbing. Trying to rub everything out of my screwed-up skull.

I got a new truck and gave her the car, but things didn't improve. Every evening tempers flared and I could see the end getting closer. I couldn't forgive her for telling me on New Years Eve. Joe had told me that it had nothing to do with the holiday, just that she had wanted to get her point across and it just happened to be that night. No matter what the explanation, it didn't sit right with me.

The following month, Sandy phoned and asked if I'd come and play guitar and sing at his fiftieth birthday party. He didn't know what had happened. I told him and he was floored.

"Is it okay now? Maybe coming up here for a week will give you two a break." said Sandy.

"I don't know. I'll talk it over with her. It's a mess."

"Okay bud, let me know okay. Call me back in a few days."

I told Kathy about the party and she agreed that the break may be what we needed. When it was time to leave for Tennessee that early morning, we kissed goodbye at the front door. I jumped in the truck and we both looked each other in the eyes. I had a lump in her throat and she had teary eyes. I knew we both still loved each other. I felt we were healing from the nightmare of New Years Eve.

But returning home was bittersweet. I couldn't wait to get home so I drove straight through and returned Sunday night instead of Monday morning. She had decided it wasn't going to work. We talked and again my temper went out of control. That next day I drove myself to the Vet Center. Joe took me right in.

"Joe, it's not working. She wants her own place. A divorce, I don't know. I just can't believe this is happening to us."

"I know, calm down Phil. If she is determined to get her own place, let her. You can't stop her. You need to start thinking of you now. Don't get sick, I worry about you."

"I know; I'll be okay. Shit, this is worse than 'Nam!"

"I hear ya brother. Many guys go through this. Look, we heard about the Bronze Star. We're having a ceremony here next month. You do deserve it."

"I don't feel like a damn hero. I feel like a damn failure."

"You must accept the award for all the guys who fought and died in Vietnam with you, okay?"

I agreed and again we shook hands and hugged. I headed home consumed with emptiness and dread. I never knew what to expect when I went home.

✪ ✪ ✪

KATHY MOVED OUT. I couldn't believe what was happening. I even helped her move. We seemed friendly at times, but then I'd go off and get mad at her.

I sat in the house alone for two weeks, crying and not eating. I was tempted to drink, but resisted. I didn't trust myself. If I took a drink, I probably would have done some damage somewhere. I went to my VA counselor weekly, along with seeing Joe. They kept a tight lid on me. I was told to try and accept what had happened and to move on, but I had no feelings, I was dead inside. We filled out papers for the divorce but she wouldn't sign them. This was messing up my head more. She wanted out, but wouldn't sign the papers.

My counselor at the VA told me to get out of the house and to quit feeling sorry for myself. I did, and I made a new friend, Evelyn. We met at low points in each others lives. Evelyn had lost her husband to cancer two years before. It was nice talking to someone who wasn't tied into my past, to Vietnam. We shared our survival stories and comforted each other. I hoped that after my divorce, our relationship would grow into something more.

My moods would change though, like the wind. I resisted change and couldn't except what had happened. It took time for me to get comfortable in my new relationship. Evelyn was patient and understanding, and I needed that. I couldn't change overnight after being with Kathy for so long.

I worried about Kathy and somehow felt sorry for her— sorry because when she was still a kid I put her though the Vietnam War with me. I chose to be part of such a horrible time in our nation's history. I chose to drag Kathy through the horrors with me.

When the date was set for me to receive the Bronze Star,

Kathy asked to go.

I told her no. I was hurting too bad. I didn't want her there. The divorce hearing was set on my fifty-first birthday, January 10, 2001. I requested it be moved to the next day. I didn't need anymore anniversary dates to remember.

The hearing was at the same courthouse we had been married in.

"Do either of you have doubts about this divorce?" the judge asked.

I admitted I did, but Kathy said she had enough. She even mentioned Vietnam and that surprised me. The judge shook his head, and gave me thanks for serving.

Then all too fast it was over. The thirty years in my past had just flashed by. It was as though a section of my life had been erased. I was empty. Kathy drove the car home and I cried as she drove.

"Do you realize what just happened?" I cried.

"It'll be all right. Things happen for a reason," she said.

I think I'm still searching for that reason, but little by little I'm getting there. Finding someone to share my life with again has made the transition easier on me, but the hurt will linger a long time. For both of us.

✪ ✪ ✪

JUNE SIXTH, TWO-THOUSAND. A Sunday. Thirty years to the day that I was released from the hospital after being wounded. I woke early put on a suit and tie and drove myself to the National Guard Armory in St. Petersburg. I was very nervous. My face was showing the last few months' worth of stress. My mood was somber and loneliness overwhelmed me.

It was an off day for me. My memories bounced from Vietnam to New Years Eve. My life had reached this point that seemed to be the finish of something. And with the award it seemed maybe the end of the Vietnam era that had always haunted me. It would be closure. The recognition that was way overdue was finally here. Bittersweet, but never the less, it was here.

When I arrived at the National Guard Amory I was greeted by retired major Tom Veit, the man who helped get the award processed for me. The company stood at attention while I walked up to receive my award. I was nervous, but not as nervous as the female officer presenting me with the medal. She actually dropped it on the floor.

To make her feel at ease and lighten the moment, I whispered, "Gee, they didn't have good looking women like you when I was in the Army."

She raised a smile and her nervousness disappeared.

I accepted the award that day with pride. My daughter and her fiancé Howard were there, along with some friends. Sandy came from Tennessee. TV news reporter Peter Bernard covered the event for the local nightly news.

I was surrounded by friends, but a piece of me was missing. When it came down to it, others deserved a medal too. My wife should have shared in the honors along side of me that day. She too was a hero. She stood for all Vietnam veterans who suffered. She felt the pain and took care of me.

To this day, I regret not having my wife with me at the ceremony. I put her through the war, and yet denied her the recognition she had earned as well.

Still, the ceremony was closure on the struggles of the last ten years—no, the last thirty. The armory was filled with young soldiers lined up in formation to honor a wounded veteran. Afterwards I shook hands with each and every one.

It healed me. Despite the personal objections individuals might have to war, never again would America as a country disrespect those who fought and served and died at the government's request. There would be challenges, to be sure, but these young soldiers would not live in the darkened world I had endured.

As I left the armory, a new feeling filled my heart.

Hope.

Epilogue

I DON'T PLAN ANYMORE. Instead I take life as it comes, and not even the simplest of things goes underappreciated. I've learned the most treasured part of living is family. We must take care and nurture what we have. It's gone all too fast. It's so easy to let things go unsaid, then we wind up regretting things we didn't do.

Since the September eleventh attacks we all take life a little less for granted. We again witnessed what true heroes really are. We love this country and when Americans are pushed against a wall, they will stand and defend. Our young will fill the shoes of us old soldiers, just as we did in our war.

I'm watching the tides of the Gulf of Mexico again, as I did as a kid. It's the same water, but much has changed in my life. I enjoy writing and I've been encouraged by Evelyn to do my music again. With the music I've been able to capture some of my stolen youth. My greatest joy is having the privilege to watch my daughter pursue her dreams and ambitions. I've been down but realized I had a lot to get back up for. Michelle, my daughter, gave me that strength and Evelyn's love has given me the courage to pursue a happier life. Kathy and I have become friends again, and share in our daughter's life. Even apart, we're still a family.

I'm still dealing with my health problems, but I understand the reason for the pain. I get emotional when I hear another US soldier was killed in Iraq. Things haven't changed that much. I'm afraid there will be another Wall. I had hoped we'd never have to raise another monument to our fallen heroes.

I want to believe my past thirty years was a good part of my life and I'll look back on it without regret. I have many more years to look forward to. I have the chance to be happy. My friends whose names are on The Wall in D.C. don't. I'll always keep that in mind every time I'm down. But for now, the magic carpet ride has slowed down and I'm learning to accept change and be grateful for the blessings in my life.

Yes, I faced The Wall. When I did, I started to face the demands of Vietnam. I knew eventually I'd have to face my war experience in order to move on. Facing The Wall probably changed the course of my life, as did the Vietnam War. I feel as though I've traveled full circle. I'm ready to start another circle. I'm sure it will have its highs and lows as well, but I'll endure. It's the love and good stuff that will lead me through the rest of my life. And, for what it's worth, I'm proud to say I was a soldier and I was finally respected. As for tomorrow?—I think I'll do just fine.

At least I've got the chance.

✪ THE END ✪

About The Author

PHIL FERRAZANO WAS born in Long Island, New York in 1950. His family moved to Clearwater, Florida in 1960 and it's been his home ever since. After graduating from Clearwater High in 1968, he was drafted into the US Army in 1969. He served as an infantry soldier with the 9th Division and was involved in the Cambodian offensive in 1970. For his actions in Cambodia he was awarded the Purple Heart and the Bronze Star with V device.

Additional decorations include the Army Commendation medal, the Combat Infantry Badge, the Republic of Vietnam Service medal with three Bronze Stars, the Good Conduct medal, the Cross of Gallantry Vietnam, and of course, the Vietnam Campaign Medal.

His ordeal in Vietnam and with the VA has been featured on various news programs, in newspapers like the St. Petersburg Times, as well as *Vietnam Magazine*. He also appeared in Lee Andresen's book *Battle Notes: Music Of The Vietnam War*.

Phil enjoys music and writing. In honor of his comrades on The Wall, Phil has produced a CD of original songs entitled, *Reflections: Vietnam Veterans Remembered*. He currently lives on the west coast of Florida, not far from where he was raised. After Vietnam he says, "There's no place like home."

Phil loves to hear from his readers. You can reach the author at Phil@FacingTheWall.com. You can visit his website at http://www.FacingTheWall.com.

Reflections: Vietnam Veterans Remembered
Songs From The Heart

Now you can enjoy the music Phil Ferrazano wrote after his emotional trip to The Wall in Washington D.C. in 1998.

Songs include:

- **Touching Your Name** - A veteran remembers those he lost in Vietnam.
- **Lovely Angels on a Wall** - In honor of the eight female Army nurses engraved on The Wall.
- **Joe Plays His Guitar** - Written by my friend Devon Anderson.
- **Mekong River, I'm Going Home** - A soldier says goodbye to a thing of beauty, tainted by years of war.
- **Sons & Daughters** - Dedicated to the Sons & Daughters In-Touch Program which connects children whose fathers died in Vietnam with those who knew them. A loving daughter leaves mementos at The Wall to include her dad in every important event in her life.

Song samples can be found at www.FacingTheWall.com.

To order, send check or money order for $10.00 plus $2.00 s&h in the U.S., or $5.00 s&h outside the U.S. to:

Phil Ferrazano
1472 Canterbury Drive
Clearwater, FL 33756

Include the information below with your order:

Name: _____

Address: _____

City, State, Zip, Country: _____

Phone:_____ Email: _____

A portion of the proceeds from the sales of this CD will be donated to Veteran's organizations.

LogOut by J.L. Hansen
Corporate life can kill you. Literally.

Sick building syndrome plagued computer security expert Julie Wynn. Simply walking through the gleaming glass doors of ExecuSource Financial buckled her stomach and tightened her ribs around her lungs. Any weekday brought watery eyes, a runny nose, and headaches that drove roofing nails into her skull. Each tick of the time clock intensified her misery. Her life as a corporate slave was killing her.

One by one her friends end up in the hospital with debilitating symptoms the doctors can't explain. But when Julie tries to put her health first and quit, her boss threatens to blame her for an impending multi-million dollar lawsuit from the Business Software Alliance.

To save herself, her career, and her friends, Julie must find the source of the mysterious epidemic threatening ExecuSource. Along the way she confronts scheming inside traders, malicious blackmailers, depraved kidnappers, and a category five hurricane heading straight for Tampa Bay.

A corporate slave technothriller set in Tampa, Florida.

ABOUT THE AUTHOR
J.L. Hansen is the pen name of freelance writer Janice Strand, the editor for Phil Ferrazano's *Facing The Wall: An Infantryman's Post-Vietnam Memoir*. Visit her website at http://www.JLHansen.com.

TO ORDER ONLINE
Hardcover available from Mundania Press, LLC - http://www.Mundania.com. Trade paperback and e-book available from Hard Shell Word Factory - http://www.HardShell.com.

TO ORDER BY MAIL
To order the trade paperback by mail, send check or money order for $14.95 plus $3.85 shipping and handling (total=$18.80) to:

Hard Shell Word Factory
P.O. Box 161
Amherst Junction, WI 54407

Reference "*LogOut* ISBN 0-7599-3937-3." Include your name, address, and phone number with your order.

CPSIA information can be obtained at www.ICGtesting.com
Printed in the USA
LVOW10s0737240715

447490LV00002B/3/P